Q & As
FOR THE
PMBOK® GUIDE
FOURTH EDITION
FOURTH EDITION

D1308097

Edited by Frank T. Anbari, PhD, PMP

Q & As
FOR THE
PMBOK®
GUIDE
FOURTH EDITION

Edited by Frank T. Anbari, PhD, PMP

FSC
www.fsc.org
MIX
Paper from
responsible sources
FSC® C015782

Q & As for the PMBOK® Guide—Fourth Edition

ISBN: 978-1-933890-75-3

Published by: Project Management Institute, Inc.
                  14 Campus Boulevard
                  Newtown Square, Pennsylvania 19073-3299 USA.
                  Phone: +610-356-4600
                  Fax: +610-356-4647
                  E-mail: customercare@pmi.org
                  Internet: www.PMI.org

PMI Publications welcomes corrections and comments on its
books. Please feel free to send comments on typographical,
formatting, or other errors. Simply make a copy of the relevant
page of the book, mark the error, and send it to: Book Editor, PMI
Publications, 14 Campus Boulevard, Newtown Square, PA 19073-
3299 USA.

To inquire about discounts for resale or educational purposes,
please contact the PMI Book Service Center.

PMI Book Service Center
P.O. Box 932683, Atlanta, GA 31193-2683 USA
Phone: 1-866-276-4764 (within the U.S. or Canada) or
+1-770-280-4129 (globally)
Fax: +1-770-280-4113
E-mail: info@bookorders.pmi.org

10 9 8 7 6

Table of Contents

Introduction

In the rapidly growing, fast-changing, and highly competitive world of project management, more and more professionals are recognizing the importance of developing a deeper understanding of the generally accepted knowledge and practice of the project management profession. *Q & As for the PMBOK® Guide Fourth Edition* facilitates this goal by offering 200 multiple choice questions and answers that cover key themes and concepts of project management. This helpful book addresses the project management Knowledge Areas and processes of *A Guide to the Project Management Body of Knowledge (PMBOK® Guide) – Fourth Edition*, the Project Management Institute's global standard. Answers are provided in the back of the book and include references and excerpted text from the *PMBOK® Guide – Fourth Edition*, to enhance the reader's breadth and depth of knowledge. The handy pocket size of *Q & As for the PMBOK® Guide Fourth Edition* makes it convenient to refer to the book anytime, anywhere.

Many people were instrumental in putting together this book and its predecessor publications, *PMBOK Q & A*, *Q & As for the PMBOK® Guide 2000 Edition*, and *Q & As for the PMBOK® Guide Third Edition*. The Project Management Institute (PMI) would like to thank the following contributors to *PMBOK Q & A*: Lewis Ireland, Walter Taylor, Jim Downer, Terry Borovec, Nancy Krajcar, Marylyn Longo, Sue Spengler, Ahmet Taspinar, Joe Abron, Bob Thompson, Francis Hartman, Dana Littlefield, David Overbye, and James Henderson, along with former PMI staff members James S. Pennypacker, Bobby R. Hensley, Toni D. Knott, Allison S. Boone, and Mark S. Parker. PMI would like to thank the following contributors to *Q & As for the PMBOK® Guide 2000*

Edition: Frank T. Anbari and Kate Pechter, along with PMI staff members Steven L. Fahrenkrog, Kristen L. Wright, Richard Schwartz, and Danielle Moore. PMI would also like to thank the following contributors to *Q & As for the PMBOK® Guide Third Edition*: Frank T. Anbari and Donald F. Martin, along with PMI staff members Steven L. Fahrenkrog, Dottie Nichols, Richard Schwartz, and Barbara Walsh.

Finally, PMI would like to thank the following contributors to *Q & As for the PMBOK® Guide Fourth Edition*: Frank T. Anbari, PhD, PMP (who again provided significant book content and editorial contributions), along with the following PMI staff members:

Steven L. Fahrenkrog, PMP • VP Regional Development
John Zlockie • Manager, Standards
Donn Greenberg • Manager, Publications
Kristin L. Vitello, Standards Project Specialist
Roberta Storer • Product Editor
Barbara Walsh • Publications Planner

The PMI team responsible for *Q & As for the PMBOK® Guide Fourth Edition* hopes that you will reinforce your knowledge and enjoy using this updated, expanded, and enhanced project management tool.

Q & As
FOR THE
PMBOK® GUIDE
FOURTH EDITION
Questions

Introduction
(Chapter 1 of the *PMBOK® Guide*)

1. A project is:

A. A set of sequential activities performed in a process or system.

B. A revenue-generating activity that needs to be accomplished while achieving customer satisfaction.

C. An ongoing endeavor undertaken to meet customer or market requirements.

D. A temporary endeavor undertaken to create a unique product, service, or result.

2. Project management is:

A. The integration of the critical path method and the Earned Value Management system.

B. The application of knowledge, skills, tools, and techniques to project activities to meet project requirements.

C. The application of knowledge, skills, wisdom, science, and art to organizational activities to achieve operational excellence.

D. A subset of most engineering and other technical disciplines.

3. Managing a project typically includes:

A. Balancing the competing project constraints including scope, quality, schedule, budget, resources, and risk.

B. Integrating requirements of profitability, low cost, and legal responsibility.

C. Implementation of software, hardware, and other systems to enhance organizational efficiency.

D. Supporting human factors, communications, discipline, and performance management.

4. Portfolio management refers to:

A. Managing various contents of the project file.

B. Managing the levels of financial authority to facilitate project decision making.

C. Identifying, prioritizing, authorizing, managing, and controlling projects, programs, and other related work, to achieve specific strategic business objectives.

D. Applying resource-leveling heuristics across all the organization's projects to achieve the organization's strategic objectives.

5. Project success is measured by:

A. Degree to which the project satisfies its time and budget objectives.

B. Triple constraints of schedule, cost, and technical performance.

C. Product and project quality, timeliness, budget compliance, and degree of customer satisfaction.

D. Degree to which the project satisfies the needs for which it was undertaken and its long-term contribution to aggregate performance of the organization's portfolio.

6. A program is a:

A. Grouping of related tasks lasting one year or less.

B. Group of related projects managed in a coordinated way.

C. Project with a cost over $1 million.

D. Sequence of steps constituting a project.

7. A primary function of a project management office (PMO) is to support the project manager in a variety of ways which generally include all of the following EXCEPT:

A. Delivering specific project objectives and controlling the assigned project resources to best meet objectives of the project.

B. Managing shared resources across all projects administered by the PMO.

C. Identifying and developing project management methodology, best practices, and standards.

D. Coaching, mentoring, training, and oversight.

8. All of the following are true about projects and operations EXCEPT:

A. Operations are ongoing, repetitive, and permanent endeavors while projects are temporary endeavors.

B. Projects require project management while operations require business process management or operations management.

C. Projects can intersect with operations at various points during the product life cycle. At each point, deliverables and knowledge are transferred between the project and operations for implementation of the delivered work.

D. Projects, because of their temporary nature, cannot help achieve an organization's goals. Therefore, strategic activities in the organization can be generally addressed within the organization's normal operations.

9. The *PMBOK® Guide* is the standard for:

A. Managing all projects all of the time across all industries.

B. Managing all projects all of the time across some types of industries.

C. Managing most projects most of the time across many types of industries.

D. Managing some projects some of the time across few types of industries.

10. Enterprise environmental factors refer to both internal and external environmental factors that surround or influence a project's success. All of the following are true about these factors EXCEPT:

A. Enterprise environmental factors include organizational culture, structure, and processes.

B. Enterprise environmental factors include government or industry standards, such as regulatory agency regulations, codes of conduct, product standards, quality standards, and workmanship standards.

C. Enterprise environmental factors include project management information systems (e.g., an automated tool, such as a scheduling software tool, a configuration management system, an information collection and distribution system, or web interfaces to other online automated systems).

D. Enterprise environmental factors do not include personnel administration functions (e.g., staffing and retention guidelines, employee performance reviews and training records, overtime policy, and time tracking) because these are considered to be functions of the Human Resources department.

Project Life Cycle and Organization
(Chapter 2 of the *PMBOK® Guide*)

11. The collection of generally sequential and sometimes overlapping project phases, whose name and number are determined by the management and control needs of the organization or organizations involved in the project, is known as the:

A. Project waterfall.

B. Project life cycle.

C. Project life stages.

D. Project Management Process Groups.

12. All of the following are true about project phases and the project life cycle EXCEPT:

A. Stakeholder influences, risk, and uncertainty are greatest at the start of the project. These factors decrease over the life of the project.

B. The ability to influence the final characteristics of the project's product, without significantly impacting cost, is highest at the start of the project and decreases as the project progresses towards completion.

C. The cost of changes and correcting errors typically increases substantially as the project approaches completion.

D. Cost and staffing levels are generally steady throughout the project life cycle.

13. Which of the following is NOT true about project stakeholders?

A. They are persons or organizations that are actively supportive of the project.

B. They are persons or organizations who are actively involved in the project.

C. They are persons or organizations whose interests may be positively or negatively affected by the performance or completion of the project.

D. They are persons or organizations that may exert influence over the project, its deliverables, and the project team members.

14. In considering project stakeholders, the project management team must do all of the following EXCEPT:

A. Identify both internal and external stakeholders.

B. Determine project requirements and expectations of all parties involved.

C. As much as possible, create conflicts among various stakeholders to allow the project team to get its work done.

D. Manage the influence of the various stakeholders in relation to the project requirements to ensure a successful outcome.

15. Organizational cultures and styles:

A. Are generally similar and manifest in similar ways.

B. Are generally similar but manifest in different ways.

C. Have no impact on a clearly defined project.

D. May have a strong influence on a project's ability to meet its objectives.

16. The project manager has the greatest level of independence and authority in a _____ organization.

A. Strong matrix

B. Weak matrix

C. Projectized

D. Functional

17. The project manager has the lowest level of authority in a _____ organization:

A. Functional

B. Weak matrix

C. Strong matrix

D. Projectized

18. A project coordinator may typically be found in a _____ organization.

A. Projectized

B. Strong matrix

C. Weak matrix

D. Balanced matrix

19. The project manager is more likely to have a full-time role in a _____ organization:

A. Functional

B. Weak matrix

C. Projectized

D. Small capitalization

20. A common title for the project manager's role in a projectized organization is:

A. Project Manager.

B. Project Coordinator.

C. Project Coach.

D. Project Expediter.

21. All of the following are generally true about the project management office (PMO) EXCEPT:

A. It may provide project management support functions.

B. It should be generally located in a centralized, bright, well-ventilated area.

C. It may provide training, mentoring, and coaching of project managers.

D. It may actually be responsible for the direct management of a project.

22. Different or conflicting objectives among project stakeholders:

A. Should be encouraged.

B. Should be ignored.

C. Can make it difficult for project managers to manage stakeholder expectations.

D. Generally make it easy for project managers to manage stakeholder expectations.

23. For a large, complex project with cross-functional project needs, the following organizational structure gives considerable authority to the project manager:

A. Strong matrix organization.

B. Balanced matrix organization.

C. Weak matrix.

D. Functional organization.

24. All of the following statements about the level of authority of the project manager are true EXCEPT:

A. In a functional organization, the project manager has little or no authority.

B. In weak matrices, the project manager role is more that of a coordinator or expediter than that of a manager.

C. The balanced matrix organization does not provide the project manager with the full authority over the project and project funding.

D. In a strong matrix organization, authority of the project manager is limited.

25. All of the following statements about the project life cycle and the product life cycle are true EXCEPT:

A. The product life cycle consists of generally sequential, non-overlapping product phases determined by the manufacturing and control need of the organization.

B. The last product life cycle phase for a product is generally the product's retirement.

C. Generally, a product life cycle is contained within the project life cycle.

D. Generally, a project life cycle is contained within one or more product life cycles.

Project Management Processes for a Project

(Chapter 3 of the *PMBOK® Guide*)

26. The five Project Management Process Groups are:

A. Planning, Checking, Directing, Monitoring, and Recording.

B. Initiating, Planning, Executing, Monitoring and Controlling, and Closing.

C. Planning, Executing, Directing, Closing, and Delivering.

D. Initiating, Executing, Monitoring, Evaluating, and Closing.

27. Project Management Process Groups are:

A. Overlapping activities that occur throughout the project.

B. Overlapping activities that generally occur at the same level of intensity within each phase of the project.

C. Generally discrete, one-time events.

D. Discrete, repetitive events that occur generally at the same level of intensity throughout each phase of the project.

28. The linkages between Project Management Process Groups are best described by the following:

A. The work breakdown structure links Process Groups.

B. Process Groups are linked by their planned objectives—the summary objective of one often becomes the detailed action plan for another.

C. Process Groups are linked by the outputs they produce—the output of one process generally becomes an input to another process or is a deliverable of the project.

D. There are no significant links between discrete Process Groups.

29. The relationship between Project Management Process Groups and project life cycle phases is best described by the following:

A. They are unrelated, incompatible concepts.

B. They are the same concept described by different terms to satisfy application area extensions.

C. Phases cross Process Groups such that closing one Process Group provides an input to initiating the next phase.

D. Process Groups interact within each project phase and are normally repeated for each phase.

30. For a project to be successful, the project team must generally do all of the following EXCEPT:

A. Comply with requirements to meet stakeholder needs and expectations.

B. Balance the competing demands of scope, time, cost, quality, resources, and risk to produce the specified product, service, or result.

C. Apply knowledge, skills, and processes within the Project Management Process Groups uniformly to meet the project objectives.

D. Select appropriate processes within the Project Management Process Groups to meet the project objectives.

31. All of the following are characteristics of Project Management Process Groups EXCEPT:

A. Project Management Process Groups are linked by the outputs they produce.

B. The Process Groups are seldom either discrete or one-time events; they are overlapping activities that occur throughout the project.

C. All of the processes are generally needed on all projects, and all of their interactions apply to all projects or project phases.

D. When a project is divided into phases, the Process Groups are invoked as appropriate to effectively drive the project to completion in a controlled manner.

32. The Initiating Process Group consists of the processes performed to:

A. Define a new project or a new phase of an existing project by obtaining authorization to start the project or phase.

B. Deploy risk mitigation strategies to enhance the likelihood of project success.

C. Establish and describe the need for a project selection process.

D. Approve the market analysis to ensure resolution of potential contract disputes.

33. Invoking the Initiating processes at the start of each phase:

A. Is wasteful and should be avoided whenever possible.

B. Helps keep the project focused on the business need the project was undertaken to address.

C. Helps ensure that the project continues regardless of changes in the success criteria.

D. Helps ensure continuous employment of project team members even if the project is unlikely to satisfy the business need that it was undertaken to address.

34. Identifying quality requirements and/or standards for the project and product and documenting how the project will demonstrate compliance should be developed in the:

A. Conceptual phase.

B. Planning process.

C. Project implementation phase.

D. Identify Risks process.

35. The schedule control process for a project:

A. Focuses on starting the project earlier than scheduled to help mitigate schedule risk.

B. Is necessary for monitoring the status of the project and managing changes to the schedule baseline.

C. Is concerned mainly with activities that are on the critical path.

D. Should focus entirely on activities that are difficult to carry out.

36. All of the following processes are performed in the Executing Process Group EXCEPT:

A. Completing the work defined in the project management plan to satisfy the project specifications.

B. Coordinating people and resources in accordance with the project management plan.

C. Integrating and performing the activities of the project in accordance with the project management plan.

D. Finalizing all activities across all Project Management Process Groups to formally complete appropriate project phases or contractual obligations.

Project Integration Management
(Chapter 4 of the *PMBOK® Guide*)

37. Which process is included in Project Integration Management?

A. Develop project management plan.

B. Control scope definition.

C. Review scope verification.

D. Conduct procurement surveillance.

38. All of the following are characteristics of the project charter EXCEPT:

A. It formally authorizes a project or a phase.

B. Projects are authorized by someone external to the project at a level that is appropriate to funding the project that either creates the project charter or delegates that duty to the project manager.

C. It is used primarily to request bids for a project or specific phases of a project.

D. It provides the project manager with the authority to apply resources to project activities.

39. Which of the following is NOT true about tools and techniques of integrated change control?

A. Include expert judgment.

B. Include change control meetings.

C. A change control board is responsible for meeting and reviewing change requests and approving or rejecting them.

D. Include project plan updates.

40. Which of the following is an acceptable cause for "re-baselining" a $10 million project?

A. The client has approved an addition to the scope of the project with a $150,000 budget increase and a 2-week extension of the scheduled completion.

B. The contractor's company has instituted a quality assurance program in which it has pledged to spend one million dollars during the next year.

C. The productivity in the Design Department is lower than estimated, which has resulted in 1,000 additional hours over what was budgeted and a forecasted 2-week delay of the scheduled completion.

D. The Engineering Department of the performing organization has converted to a new $250,000 CAD system.

41. A configuration management system with integrated change control provides a standardized, effective, and efficient way to centrally manage approved changes and baselines within a project. Configuration control is focused on:

A. The identification and correction of problems arising in functional areas of project implementation.

B. The specification of both the deliverables and the processes while change control is focused on identifying, documenting, and controlling changes to the project and the product baselines.

C. Testing new systems.

D. Identifying, documenting, and controlling changes to the project and the product baselines while change control is focused on the specification of both the deliverables and the processes.

42. A change control board (CCB) is:

A. A formally constituted group of stakeholders responsible for ensuring that only a minimal amount of changes occur on the project.

B. A formal or an informal group of stakeholders that has oversight of project execution.

C. A formally constituted group of stakeholders responsible for reviewing, evaluating, approving, delaying, or rejecting changes to a project, with all decisions and recommendations being recorded.

D. A dashboard that provides integrated information to help control changes to cost, schedule, and specifications throughout the life of the project.

43. The Perform Integrated Change Control process includes all of the following change management activities EXCEPT:

A. Reviewing, analyzing, and approving change requests promptly, which is essential, as a slow decision may negatively affect time, cost, or the feasibility of a change.

B. Monitoring changes in resource leveling heuristics to ensure efficient resource utilization throughout the life cycle of the project.

C. Maintaining the integrity of baselines by releasing only approved changes for incorporation into the project management plan and project documents.

D. Coordinating changes across the entire project (e.g., a proposed schedule change will often affect cost, risk, quality, and staffing).

44. All of the following are characteristics of the project management information system (PMIS) EXCEPT:

A. It is part of the enterprise environmental factors.

B. It provides access to an automated tool, such as a scheduling software tool, a configuration management system, an information collection and distribution system, or web interfaces to other online automated systems.

C. It is used during the Direct and Manage Project Execution effort.

D. It is used by the project manager and the project management team primarily to generate presentations to key stakeholders.

45. Outputs of the Monitor and Control Project Work process include all of the following EXCEPT:

A. Change requests.

B. Project management plan updates.

C. Project document updates.

D. Final product, service, or result transition.

46. Actions and activities necessary to satisfy completion or exit criteria for the phase or project and to transfer the project's products, services, or results to the next phase or to production and/or operations are addressed:

A. As part of the Close Project or Phase process.

B. Following the plan outlined in the Quality Management process.

C. As requested by senior executives.

D. As the last step in project management.

Project Scope Management
(Chapter 5 of the *PMBOK® Guide*)

47. All of the following are true about the project scope management plan EXCEPT:

A. It provides guidance on how project scope will be defined, documented, managed, and controlled.

B. It provides guidance on how project scope will be verified.

C. It may be formal or informal, highly detailed, or broadly framed, based upon the needs of the project.

D. It is separate from the project management plan.

48. Collect Requirements is the process of defining and documenting stakeholders' needs to meet the project objectives. All of the following are true about this process EXCEPT:

A. The project's success is directly influenced by the care taken in capturing and managing project and product requirements.

B. Requirements include the quantified and documented needs and expectations of the sponsor, customer, and other stakeholders.

C. Requirements become the foundation of the WBS. Cost, schedule, and quality planning are all built upon these requirements.

D. The development of requirements begins with an analysis of the information contained in the risk register.

49. All of the following are true about the project scope statement EXCEPT:

A. It is an output of the Verify Scope process.

B. It describes, in detail, the project's deliverables and the work required to create those deliverables.

C. It provides a common understanding of the project scope among project stakeholders.

D. It may contain explicit scope exclusions that can assist in managing stakeholder expectations.

50. All of the following are true about the Control Scope process EXCEPT:

A. Control Scope is the process of monitoring the status of the project and product scope and managing changes to the scope baseline.

B. Project scope control is used to manage the actual changes when they occur and is integrated with the other control processes.

C. Scope changes can be avoided by developing clear and concise specifications and enforcing strict adherence to them.

D. Scope control includes determining the cause and degree of variance relative to the scope baseline and deciding whether corrective or preventive action is required.

51. Which of the following statements is true about the work breakdown structure (WBS)?

A. The WBS is a deliverable-oriented hierarchical decomposition of the work to be executed by the project team to accomplish the project objectives and create the required deliverables.

B. The WBS is an unstructured list of project activities in chart form.

C. The WBS is the same as the organizational breakdown structure (OBS).

D. The WBS is the bill of materials (BOM) needed to accomplish the project objectives and create the required deliverables.

52. The following is an example of a constraint associated with the project scope that limits the team's options in scope definition:

A. A predefined budget.

B. The threat of a strike by a subcontractor.

C. Existing relationships with sellers, suppliers, or others in the supply chain.

D. The method used to measure project performance.

53. An input to the Define Scope process is:

A. The type of contract detail language.

B. Project Charter.

C. Work breakdown structure (WBS).

D. Decomposition.

54. What is the WBS typically used for?

A. To organize and define the total scope of the project.

B. To identify the logical person to be project sponsor.

C. To define the level of reporting that the seller provides the buyer.

D. As a record of when work elements are assigned to individuals.

55. The following is true about the WBS:

A. The WBS is another term for the bar (Gantt) chart.

B. Each descending level of the WBS represents an increasingly detailed definition of the project work.

C. Work not in the WBS is usually defined in the scope statement of the project.

D. The WBS shows only the critical path activities.

56. An output of the Define Scope process is:

A. Work breakdown structure (WBS).

B. Resource breakdown structure (RBS).

C. Project scope statement.

D. Scope and schedule delays control plan.

57. Which of the following is true about the Verify Scope process?

A. It is the process of formalizing acceptance of the completed project deliverables.

B. Is not necessary if the project completes on time and within budget.

C. Occurs primarily when revisions or changes are made to project scope.

D. Scope verification is primarily concerned with correctness of the deliverables, while quality control is primarily concerned with acceptance of the deliverables and meeting the quality requirements specified for the deliverables.

58. Which of the following is not an output of the Control Scope process?

A. Work performance measurements.

B. Change requests.

C. Project document updates.

D. Accepted deliverables.

Project Time Management
(Chapter 6 of the *PMBOK® Guide*)

59. The Project Time Management processes include:

A. Activity Definition, Activity Sequencing, Activity Execution, Activity Duration Estimation, and Activity Control.

B. Define Activities, Sequence Activities, Estimate Activity Resources, Estimate Activity Durations, Develop Schedule, and Control Schedule.

C. Identify Activities, Develop Schedule, Execute Activities, Control Activities, and Monitor Schedule Results.

D. Determine Activities, Estimate Activity Durations, Develop Schedule, Implement Activities, and Report Activity Results.

60. In rolling wave planning:

A. Focus is maintained on long-term objectives, allowing near-term objectives to be rolled out as part of the ongoing wave of activities.

B. The work to be accomplished in the near term is planned in detail and future work is planned at a higher level of the WBS.

C. The work far in the future is planned in detail for WBS components that are at a low level of the WBS.

D. A wave of detailed activities is planned during strategic planning to ensure that WBS deliverables and project milestones are achieved.

61. The precedence diagramming method (PDM):

A. Uses boxes or rectangles to represent activities. Therefore, it is also called activity-on-node (AON).

B. Uses a probabilistic approach to scheduling project activities.

C. Is a time-phased graphical representation of the arrow diagramming method (ADM) and shows durations of project activities as well as their dependencies.

D. Is more accurate than the critical path method for scheduling when there are uncertainties about the durations of project activities.

62. The duration of the activity is affected by all of the following EXCEPT:

A. The estimated activity resource requirements.

B. The resources assigned to the activity.

C. The availability of the resources assigned to the activity.

D. Using the precedence diagramming method (PDM) for scheduling activities instead of using the Critical Path Method (CPM).

63. The "fast tracking" method of schedule compression involves:

A. The use of industrial engineering techniques to improve productivity, thereby finishing the project earlier than originally planned.

B. Performing in parallel activities that are normally performed in sequence, which may result in rework and increased risk.

C. Going on a "mandatory overtime schedule" to complete the project on schedule or earlier if possible.

D. Assigning "dedicated teams" to critical path activities to achieve project schedule objectives.

64. An example of a mandatory dependency, as opposed to a discretionary dependency, is:

A. Project A, the company's participation in a pump industry trade show, depends on the successful completion of Project B, which is building the prototype pump that is going to be displayed.

B. To start design only after completion and approval of all project requirements.

C. For the shrink-wrapping on the finished box of software to depend on enclosing the manual and software first.

D. To schedule the final testing activity of a new computer model to start seventy-two hours after the start of the mandatory seventy-two hour "burn-in" period.

65. Inputs to the Define Activities process are:

A. Work breakdown structure, project schedule, and network diagram.

B. Project schedule, progress reports, and change requests.

C. Project network diagram, constraints, and assumptions.

D. Scope baseline, enterprise environmental factors, and organizational process assets.

66. A schedule compression technique to determine how to obtain the greatest amount of compression for the least incremental cost is called:

A. Crashing.

B. Program evaluation and review technique (PERT).

C. Precedence diagramming method (PDM).

D. Fast tracking.

67. Bar charts show:

A. The level of effort for an activity.

B. Activity start and end dates, as well as expected durations.

C. Availability of resources assigned to perform project activities.

D. Relative priority of activities.

68. The precedence diagramming method (PDM) shows:

A. Various levels of the work breakdown structure.

B. Activities likely to be involved in project integration and resource allocation processes.

C. The logical relationships that exist between activities.

D. The project completion date based on normal resource availability.

69. The critical path is established by calculating the following dates:

A. Start-to-start, start-to-finish, finish-to-finish, finish-to-start.

B. Early start, early finish, late start, late finish.

C. Predecessor-to-successor, predecessor-to-predecessor, successor-to-successor.

D. Primary-to-secondary, primary-to-finish, secondary-to-secondary, finish-to-finish.

70. All of the following are true about resource leveling EXCEPT:

A. It can be used to keep resource usage at a constant level during certain time periods.

B. It can often cause the original critical path to change.

C. It is used to optimize the distribution of work among resources.

D. It is used to develop a resource-based WBS.

71. The following is true about the critical chain:

A. It is a network scheduling technique that allows development of an optimum project schedule when resources are unlimited.

B. It is a schedule network analysis technique that modifies the project schedule to account for limited resources.

C. It is another name for the bar chart.

D. It is primarily used to ensure safety in major construction projects.

72. "Crashing" in time management is:

A. A schedule compression technique that typically includes reducing schedule activity durations and increasing the assignment of resources on schedule activities.

B. A schedule compression technique in which phases or activities that normally would be done in sequence are performed in parallel.

C. The timely input of data to calculate the critical path.

D. Equivalent to minimizing float in the project schedule network.

73. All of the following choices represent inputs to the Estimate Activity Resources process EXCEPT:

A. Activity list.

B. Enterprise environmental factors.

C. The actual resource cost of the last project.

D. Organizational process assets.

74. Output from the Estimate Activity Resources process includes:

A. Job descriptions of resources required for the project.

B. Salary schedules for various project human resources.

C. Identification of the types and quantities of resources required for each activity.

D. Analogous estimating of resource requirements.

75. As one of the tools and techniques of the Sequence Activities process, a lead:

A. Directs a delay in the successor activity.

B. Could be accomplished by a finish-to-start relationship with a delay time.

C. Means that the successor activity cannot start until after the predecessor is completed.

D. Allows an acceleration of the successor activity.

76. Program evaluation and review technique (PERT) uses:

A. The weighted average of the triangular distribution duration estimates to calculate the activity early finish date.

B. The weighted average of three point duration estimates to calculate the expected activity duration.

C. Dummy activities to represent logic ties.

D. Free float instead of total float in the schedule calculations.

77. Analogous duration estimating is:

A. The same as bottom-up estimating.

B. Frequently used to estimate project duration when there is a limited amount of detailed information about the project.

C. Similar to multiple duration estimating.

D. Generally more accurate than other duration estimating methods when expert judgment is used.

78. The critical chain:

A. Focuses on managing the resources applied to the project buffer and to feeding buffer activities.

B. Alters the required dependencies in the project schedule to optimize resource constraints.

C. Adds duration buffers that are work schedule activities to manage risk and maintains focus on the total float of network paths.

D. Adds duration buffers that are non-work schedule activities to manage uncertainty and focuses on managing remaining buffer durations against the remaining durations of task chains.

Project Cost Management

79. Project Cost Management includes all of the following processes EXCEPT:

A. Estimate Costs.

B. Level Resource.

C. Determine Budget.

D. Control Costs.

80. All of the following are true about cost estimates EXCEPT:

A. Cost estimates are generally expressed in units of some currency (i.e., dollars, euro, yen, etc.), although in some instances other units of measure, such as staff hours or staff days, are used.

B. Costs are estimated for all resources that will be charged to the project.

C. Information in the risk register should not be used to adjust cost estimates, because risks can be either threats or opportunities and their impact tends to balance out.

D. Cost estimates are quantitative assessments of the likely costs for resources required to complete project activities.

81. Project cost control includes all of the following EXCEPT:

A. Informing appropriate stakeholders of all approved changes and associated cost.

B. Monitoring cost performance to isolate and understand variances from the approved cost baseline.

C. Monitoring work performance against funds expended.

D. Allocating the overall estimates to individual work packages to establish a cost baseline.

82. An activity cost estimate includes all of the following resource categories EXCEPT:

A. Labor.

B. Materials.

C. Equipment.

D. Time shortages.

83. Parametric estimating involves:

A. Defining cost or duration parameters of the project life cycle.

B. Calculating individual cost and duration estimates for each work package and integrating them to obtain the total cost or duration of the project.

C. Using a statistical relationship between historical data and other variables to calculate an estimate for activity parameters, such as cost, budget, and duration.

D. Using the actual cost or duration of a previous similar project to estimate the cost or duration of the current project.

84. Analogous cost estimating:

A. Integrates bottom-up estimating techniques with relevant statistical relationship to estimate the cost of the current project.

B. Relies on the actual cost of previous, similar projects as the basis for estimating the cost of the current project.

C. Is used most frequently in the later phases of a project.

D. Summarizes estimates for individual work packages to estimate the cost of the current project.

85. **Which of the following represents processes concerned with establishing and controlling the cost baseline?**

A. Plan Resources and Contain Costs.

B. Estimate Costs, Develop Budget, and Adhere to Baseline.

C. Determine Budget and Control Costs.

D. Resource Planning, Cost Estimating, and Cost Control.

86. **Consider the following cumulative measures:**

$$BAC = 200$$
$$AC = 120$$
$$EV = 80$$
$$CPI = 0.666$$

Predicting that all future work will be accomplished at the budgeted rate, the estimate at completion (EAC) is:

A. 120.

B. 160.

C. 200.

D. 240.

87. Consider the following cumulative measures:

$BAC = 200$
$AC = 120$
$EV = 80$
$CPI = 0.666$

Assuming that what the project has experienced to date can be expected to continue in the future, the estimate at completion (EAC) is:

A. 220.

B. 240.

C. 300.

D. 320.

88. The cost performance baseline has all of the following characteristics EXCEPT:

A. It is an authorized time-phased budget at completion (BAC) used to measure, monitor, and control overall cost performance on the project.

B. It shows the actual cost expenditures throughout the life of the project.

C. It is developed as a summation of the approved budgets by time period.

D. It is typically displayed in the form of an S-curve.

89. The estimate at completion (EAC) is typically based on:

A. The earned value (EV) and the actual cost for work completed (AC).

B. The cost performance index (CPI) and the cost variance (CV).

C. The actual costs incurred for work completed (AC) and the cumulative cost performance index (CPI).

D. The actual costs incurred for work completed (AC), and the estimate to complete (ETC) the remaining work.

90. The cost management plan has all of the following characteristics EXCEPT:

A. It is based on the project cost estimates and is separate from the project plan.

B. It may specify variance thresholds for monitoring cost performance to indicate an agreed-upon amount of variation to be allowed before some action needs to be taken.

C. It may be formal or informal, highly detailed or broadly framed, based upon the needs of the project.

D. It sets out the format and establishes the criteria for planning, structuring, estimating, budgeting, and controlling project costs.

91. **Your earned value management analysis indicates that your project is falling behind its baseline schedule. You know this because the cumulative EV is much:**

A. Higher than the cumulative AC.

B. Higher than the cumulative PV.

C. Lower than the cumulative PV.

D. Lower than the cumulative CPI.

92. **Which of the following cumulative measures indicates that your project is about 9% under budget?**

A. The cumulative AC was 100, and the cumulative EV was 110.

B. The cumulative PV was 100, and the cumulative AC was 110.

C. The cumulative AC was 110, and the cumulative EV was 100.

D. The cumulative EV was 100, and the cumulative PV was 110.

93. Earned value management (EVM) is a commonly used:

A. Analysis of the value of the equipment that has been installed as of the status date.

B. Analysis of the sum of the labor costs, which have been incurred on the project to date.

C. Method of project performance measurement.

D. Method of measuring the amount of money that has been spent to date.

94. During the sixth monthly update on a ten-month, $300,000 project, the earned value management analysis shows that the cumulative PV is $190,000, the cumulative AC is $120,000, and the cumulative EV is $150,000. In planning its action, the project management team can conclude all of the following from these measures EXCEPT:

A. Less has been accomplished than was planned.

B. Less has been spent than planned.

C. Continuing performance at the same efficiency with no management intervention, the project will probably be completed behind schedule and under budget.

D. Continuing performance at the same efficiency with no management intervention, the project will probably be completed ahead of schedule and over budget.

95. In earned value management, the cost variance is equal to:

A. EV minus PV.

B. EV minus AC.

C. AC minus EV.

D. PV minus EV.

96. Earned value (EV) involves all of the following EXCEPT:

A. Value of work performed expressed in terms of the approved budget assigned to that work for an activity or work breakdown structure component.

B. Actual cost for an activity or work breakdown structure component.

C. Budgeted cost of work performed.

D. Budgeted amount for the work actually completed.

97. If cumulative PV = 100, cumulative EV = 98, and cumulative AC = 104, the project is likely to be:

A. Ahead of schedule.

B. Headed for a cost overrun.

C. Operating at project cost projections.

D. Under budget at completion.

Cumulative data for questions 98–99:

Item	PV	AC	EV
1	10,000	11,000	10,000
2	9,000	8000	7,000
3	8,000	8,000	8,000
4	7,000	7,000	5,000

98. Which item is MOST over budget?

A. Item 1

B. Item 2

C. Item 3

D. Item 4

99. Which item has the LOWEST SPI?

A. Item 1

B. Item 2

C. Item 3

D. Item 4

Project Quality Management

100. **Understanding, evaluating, defining, and managing expectations are essential to satisfying:**

   A. Customer requirements.

   B. The scope statement.

   C. Upper management.

   D. Functional requirements.

101. **One of the fundamental tenets of modern quality management states that:**

   A. Quality is planned and inspected in.

   B. Quality does not cost.

   C. Quality is planned, designed, and built in—not inspected in.

   D. Quality requires constant inspection.

102. **All of the following are primary benefits of meeting quality requirements EXCEPT:**

   A. Less rework.

   B. Higher productivity.

   C. Lower costs.

   D. Fewer change orders.

103. Inputs to quality control include all of the following EXCEPT:

A. Project management plan.

B. Quality checklists.

C. Work performance measurements.

D. PERT chart.

104. Design of experiments (DOE) is a statistical method used to:

A. Determine how various elements of a project interrelate.

B. Identify which factors may influence specific variables of a product or process under development or in production.

C. Establish a standard by which to measure project performance.

D. Compare actual or planned project practices to those of other projects.

105. The quality management plan provides input to _____ and includes quality control, quality assurance, and continuous process improvement approaches for the project.

A. The overall project management plan.

B. The WBS.

C. The project scope.

D. External project stakeholders.

106. Perform Quality Assurance is the process of:

A. Applying planned, systematic quality activities to ensure effective policing and conformance of the project team to approved specifications.

B. Providing the project team and stakeholders with standards by which project performance is measured.

C. Auditing the quality requirements and the results from quality control measurements to ensure appropriate quality standards and operational definitions are used.

D. Assuring the implementation of appropriate specifications, which generally results in reducing the probability of the project being completed on schedule.

107. A _____ is a specific type of histogram, ordered by frequency of occurrence, which shows how many defects were generated by type or category of identified cause.

A. PERT chart.

B. Bar chart.

C. Network diagram.

D. Pareto chart.

108. Cost of quality includes all of the following EXCEPT:

A. Preventing nonconformance to requirements.

B. Appraising the product or service for conformance to requirements.

C. Failing to meet requirements.

D. Operating computers required for the project.

109. Due to the temporary nature of a project, the _____ may choose to invest in product quality improvement, especially defect prevention and appraisal:

A. Sponsoring organization.

B. Project management team.

C. Executive management team.

D. Project quality function deployment (QFD) organization.

110. Tools and techniques of the Perform Quality Control process include all of the following EXCEPT:

A. Flowcharting.

B. Pareto chart.

C. Control charts.

D. Quality control tendency charts.

111. Project Quality Management includes the processes and activities of the performing organization that determine quality policies, objectives, and responsibilities so that:

A. The project will satisfy the needs for which it was undertaken.

B. Process capability will be improved.

C. Product and service results will be controlled.

D. Project team performance will meet standards.

112. Quality and grade are not the same. A fundamental distinction is that:

A. Grade is a category assigned to products or services having the same functional use but different technical characteristics.

B. A quality level that fails to meet quality requirements may not be a problem; low grade is always a problem.

C. Delivering the required levels of quality is not included in the responsibilities of the project manager and the project team.

D. Delivering the required levels of grade is not included in the responsibilities of the project manager and the project team.

113. Control charts have all of the following characteristics EXCEPT:

A. They are used to determine whether or not a process is stable or has predictable performance.

B. They are used to monitor various types of output variables.

C. They are used to illustrate how various factors might be linked to potential problems or effects.

D. They are used to illustrate how a process behaves over time and when a process is subject to special cause variation, resulting in an out-of-control condition.

114. Perform Quality _____ is the process of auditing the quality requirements and the results from quality control measurements to ensure appropriate quality standards and operational definitions are used.

A. Planning.

B. Assurance.

C. Improvement.

D. Benchmarking.

115. In using cost-benefit analysis in the Plan Quality process it can be noted that:

A. The primary benefit of meeting quality requirements is the reduced cost associated with project quality management activities.

B. The primary benefits of meeting quality requirements can include less rework, higher productivity, lower costs, and increased stakeholder satisfaction.

C. The primary cost of meeting quality requirements is increased rework.

D. Quality cost cannot be evaluated in relationship to the expected benefit of quality.

116. All of the following are characteristics of benchmarking EXCEPT:

A. It involves comparing actual or planned project practices to those of comparable projects to generate ideas for improvement.

B. It involves comparing actual or planned project practices to those of comparable projects to provide a basis for measuring performance.

C. It involves comparing actual or planned project practices to those of comparable projects within the performing organization or outside of it.

D. It involves comparing actual or planned project practices to those of comparable projects only within the same application area.

117. All of the following are true about Six Sigma EXCEPT:

A. It is a quality improvement initiative undertaken by the performing organization.

B. It should improve the quality of the project's management.

C. It should improve the quality of the project's product.

D. It focuses on systematically correcting defects, errors, or mistakes revealed by inspection.

Project Human Resource Management
(Chapter 9 of the *PMBOK® Guide*)

118. The major processes of Project Human Resource Management are the following:

A. Leadership, Management, Team Building, and Negotiation.

B. Develop Project Staffing Plan, Recruit Project Team, Administer Personnel Actions, and Manage Labor Relations.

C. Plan Organizational Structure, Build Project Team, Develop Communications Plan, and Manage Team Conflicts.

D. Develop Human Resource Plan, Acquire Project Team, Develop Project Team, and Manage Project Team.

119. The Acquire Project Team process includes obtaining the team necessary to complete project assignments. The enterprise environmental factors that can influence this process generally include all of the following EXCEPT:

A. Availability.

B. Political philosophy.

C. Prior experience.

D. Personnel administration policies such as those that affect outsourcing.

120. It is important that the staffing management plan addresses how team members will be released when they are no longer needed on the project for all of the following reasons EXCEPT:

A. To reduce project costs.

B. To improve morale when smooth transitions to upcoming projects are already planned.

C. To optimize the utilization of enterprise material resources.

D. To help mitigate human resource risks that may occur during or at the end of the project.

121. To be effective, recognition and rewards systems should have the following characteristics EXCEPT:

A. There should be clear criteria for rewards and a planned system for their use.

B. Recognition and rewards should be based on activities and performance under a person's control.

C. Cultural differences should be considered when determining recognition and rewards.

D. The required performance for rewards should be made unachievable for most team members, to ensure that all team members strive for excellence throughout the project.

122. Co-location is one of the tools and technique used to:

A. Plan the organizational structure.

B. Develop the project team.

C. Acquire the project team.

D. Control project human resources.

123. Tools and techniques to acquire the project team include all of the following EXCEPT:

A. Pre-assignment.

B. Acquisition.

C. Staffing management plan.

D. Negotiation.

124. The human resource plan should generally include all of the following EXCEPT:

A. Roles and responsibilities.

B. Project organization charts.

C. Staffing management plan.

D. Project interfaces.

125. All of the following are true about conflict EXCEPT:

A. It is inevitable in a project environment and should be addressed early.

B. It should be addressed usually in private.

C. It should be addressed only when it escalates and at a special team meeting.

D. It should be addressed using a direct, collaborative approach.

126. The responsibility assignment matrix (RAM) is:

A. Used for development of the project budget.

B. Developed at the activity level and used to closely link project roles and responsibilities to project network activities.

C. Used to illustrate the connections between work packages or activities and project team members. It ensures that there is only one person accountable for any one task.

D. Used to identify accountabilities in individual performance appraisals of project team members.

127. A resource histogram has all of the following characteristics EXCEPT:

A. It is generally used to show that the project has insufficient resources to be completed on schedule.

B. It is a tool for charting human resources as part of the staffing management plan.

C. It illustrates the number of hours a person, department, or entire project team will be needed each week or month over the course of the project.

D. It can include a horizontal line that represents the maximum number of hours available from a particular resource. Bars that extend beyond the maximum available hours identify the need for a resource leveling strategy.

128. Team building has all of the following characteristics EXCEPT:

A. Team-building activities can vary from a five-minute agenda item in a status review meeting to an off-site, professionally facilitated experience designed to improve interpersonal relationships.

B. Team building should be primarily considered after major conflicts within the project team, because they generally waste precious resource time and cause schedule delays.

C. Team-building strategies are particularly valuable when team members operate from remote locations without the benefit of face-to-face contact.

D. Team building is an ongoing process. To effectively manage inevitable changes in the project environment, a continued or renewed team-building effort is required.

129. Training has all of the following characteristics EXCEPT:

A. It includes all activities designed to enhance the competencies of the project team members.

B. It can be formal or informal. Examples of training methods include classroom, online, computer-based, on-the-job training from another project team member, mentoring, and coaching.

C. If project team members lack necessary management or technical skills, the project should be deemed outside the core competencies of the performing organization, outsourced, or abandoned.

D. If project team members lack necessary management or technical skills, such skills can be developed as part of the project work.

130. Effective team development strategies and activities are expected to increase the team's performance, which increases the likelihood of meeting project objectives. The evaluation of a team's effectiveness may include all of the following indicators EXCEPT:

A. Improvements in skills that allow individuals to perform assignments more effectively.

B. Improvements in competencies that help the team perform better as a team.

C. Improvements in the overall project performance as a result of increased intensity of conflict among project team members.

D. Reduced staff turnover rate.

131. During the course of many projects, negotiation is:

A. Primarily the concern of contract administration.

B. An integral part of project management and likely for staff assignments.

C. A direct result of ineffective decision-making.

D. Conducted by senior executives to increase the probability of project success.

132. Questions that may arise when planning staff acquisition for a project generally include all of the following EXCEPT:

A. Whether the human resources come from within the organization or from external, contracted sources.

B. The costs associated with each level of expertise needed for the project.

C. Senior executive compensation.

D. The extent of assistance that the organization's human resource department and functional managers can provide to the project management team.

133. Generally acknowledged techniques for resolving conflict include:

A. Soothing, compromising, collaborating, and co-locating.

B. Accepting, compromising, attacking, and separating.

C. Accommodating, compromising, forcing, and collaborating.

D. Withdrawing, forcing, elaborating, and sensitivity training.

Project Communications Management
(Chapter 10 of the *PMBOK® Guide*)

134. The major processes of Project Communications Management are:

A. Identify Stakeholders, Plan Communications, Distribute Information, Manage Stakeholder Expectations, and Report Performance.

B. Plan Communications, Plan Responses, Report Progress, Distribute Information, and Manage Stakeholders.

C. Plan Communications, Analyze Stakeholder Requirements, Distribute Information, Schedule Reporting, and Report Project Closeout.

D. Identify Stakeholders, Distribute Information, Report Changes, Update Project Documents, and Accept Project Deliverables.

135. Inputs to the Plan Communications process include:

A. Stakeholder register, stakeholder management strategy, enterprise environmental factors, and organizational process assets.

B. Stakeholder requirements, project scope statement, project budget, and project schedule.

C. Organizational structure, stakeholder analysis, project management plan, and communications barriers.

D. Stakeholder management strategy, RAM, WBS, and administrative procedures.

136. The communications management plan usually provides all of the following EXCEPT:

A. Information to be communicated, including language, format, content, and level of detail.

B. Time frame and frequency for the distribution of required information.

C. Methods or technologies used to convey the information, such as memos, e-mail, and/or press releases.

D. Memos, correspondence, reports, and documents related to the project from all stakeholders.

137. Manual filing systems, electronic databases, electronic communication tools, and web interfaces to scheduling and project management software are examples of:

A. Integrated project management information systems (IPMIS).

B. Internal communication systems.

C. Information distribution tools.

D. Project records.

138. Factors related to communication technology that can affect the project generally include all of the following EXCEPT:

A. Duration of the project.

B. Availability of technology.

C. Executive requirements.

D. Urgency of the need for information.

139. Tools and techniques for the Report Performance process generally include all of the following EXCEPT:

A. Variance analysis.

B. Decision tree analysis.

C. Forecasting methods.

D. Reporting systems.

140. As part of the communications process, the sender is responsible for:

A. Ensuring the receiver agrees with the message.

B. Confirming that the information is properly understood.

C. Presenting the information in the most favorable manner.

D. Decoding the medium correctly.

141. As part of the communications process, the receiver is responsible for:

A. Agreeing with the sender's message.

B. Pretending that the message is received only partially, to encourage further discussions.

C. Making sure that the information is received in its entirety, understood correctly, and acknowledged.

D. Specifying that a verbal message does not give insight to problem areas, and requiring that the message be reduced to writing to avoid potential confusion.

142. Information typically used to determine project communication requirements includes all of the following EXCEPT:

A. Project organization and stakeholder responsibility relationships.

B. Disciplines, departments, and specialties involved in the project.

C. Logistics of how many persons will be involved with the project and at which locations.

D. Availability of in-place technology at the project location.

143. The performance reporting process involves the periodic collection and analysis of baseline versus actual data. A simple status report might show performance information, such as percent complete, or status dashboards for:

A. Each area (i.e., scope, schedule, cost, and quality).

B. Recognition and rewards for achieving project major milestones.

C. Performance appraisals of project team members.

D. Exceptional performance by individual team member (or sub-team).

144. Communication activity has many potential dimensions that generally include all of the following EXCEPT:

A. Written, oral, and non-verbal.

B. Internal and external.

C. Conceptual and definitive.

D. Formal and informal.

145. All of the following are information distribution tools EXCEPT:

A. Hard-copy document distribution.

B. Electronic communication and conferencing tools.

C. Inputting project performance data into a spreadsheet.

D. Electronic tools for project management.

146. **The total number of potential communication channels for a project with *n* = 12 stakeholders is:**

A. $n(n-1)/2$.

B. $2n/(n-1)$.

C. $2(n-1)/n$.

D. 47 potential communications channels.

147. **Lessons learned documentation generally includes all of the following EXCEPT:**

A. The causes of issues.

B. Updates of the statement of work to reflect training and learning requirements.

C. Reasoning behind the corrective action chosen.

D. Other types of lessons learned about information distribution.

Project Risk Management
(Chapter 11 of the *PMBOK® Guide*)

148. The major processes of Project Risk Management are:

A. Plan Risk Management, Identify Risks, Assess Risks, Mitigate Risks, Transfer Risks, and Document Outcomes.

B. Identify Risks, Plan Risk Management, Evaluate Risks, Develop Risk Responses, Mitigate Risks, and Document Results.

C. Identify Risks, Perform Qualitative Risk Validation, Perform Quantitative Impact Assessment, Develop Risk Response Strategies, Document Response Strategies, and Monitor Risk Responses.

D. Plan Risk Management, Identify Risks, Perform Qualitative Risk Analysis, Perform Quantitative Risk Analysis, Plan Risk Responses, and Monitor and Control Risks.

149. Strategies typically used to deal with threats or risks that may have negative impacts on project objectives if they occur include all of the following EXCEPT:

A. Interpret.

B. Avoid.

C. Transfer.

D. Mitigate.

150. Risk transference nearly always involves:

A. Eliminating risk through beta testing.

B. Policies and procedures for a response system.

C. Accepting a lower profit if some activities overrun their budget.

D. Payment of a risk premium to the party taking on the risk.

151. To be successful, the organization should be committed to address risk management:

A. Just in time before a meeting with major stakeholders of the project.

B. Proactively and consistently throughout the project.

C. As soon as time and cost estimates are ready.

D. As early as possible in the execution phase.

152. In the Plan Risk Responses process, an accept strategy indicates that the project team has decided:

A. To agree with the project manager.

B. To eliminate a specific risk or threat, to reduce the probability and/or impact of an adverse risk event to be within acceptable threshold limits, or to pursue an opportunity actively.

C. Not to change the project management plan to deal with a risk, or is unable to identify any other suitable response strategy.

D. To purchase insurance or to require performance bonds, warranties, and guarantees.

153. The main output of the Identify Risks process is:

A. Risk register.

B. Expected monetary value of the risk events.

C. List of corrective actions.

D. Risk mitigation plan.

154. A thorough analysis of the _____ will help identify potential risks to the project.

A. Risk identification checklist based on historical information and knowledge

B. Project's change control system

C. Project's mission statement

D. Project's schedule and budget

155. All of the following are inputs to the Identify Risks process EXCEPT:

A. Risk management plan.

B. Scope baseline.

C. Work-around plan.

D. Quality management plan.

156. Outputs from the Plan Risk Responses process include all of the following EXCEPT:

A. Risk register updates.

B. Corrective actions.

C. Risk-related contract decisions.

D. Project management plan updates.

157. Tools and techniques of the Perform Quantitative Risk Analysis process are:

A. Contracting, contingency planning, alternative strategies, and insurance.

B. Interviewing, historical results, workarounds, and response development.

C. Checklists, damage control reports, standard allowances, and inspection.

D. Data gathering and representation techniques, quantitative risk analysis and modeling techniques, and expert judgment.

158. As an output of the Perform Quantitative Risk Analysis process, the risk register is updated. These updates include:

A. Prioritized list of quantified risks.

B. Probabilistic analysis of the threats to ignore and opportunities to accept.

C. Checklists, corrective actions, and quantified decision trees.

D. Direction, resources, and contingency costs.

159. **Risk impact assessment to investigate the potential effect on a project objective such as schedule, cost, quality, or performance has the following characteristics EXCEPT:**

A. Evaluation of each risk can be conducted using a probability and impact matrix that leads to rating the risks as low, moderate, or high priority.

B. Approaches used in evaluating risk impacts related to project objectives could be relative, numeric, linear, or nonlinear.

C. Usually, risk-rating rules are specified by the organization in advance of the project and can be tailored to the specific project.

D. The impact on project objectives should be assessed primarily at the end of the project, as part of the lessons learned.

160. **The outputs from the Monitor and Control Risks process include all of the following EXCEPT:**

A. Risk register updates.

B. Work breakdown structure (WBS).

C. Change requests.

D. Project management plan updates.

161. The Delphi technique has all of the following characteristics EXCEPT:

A. It is a way to reach a consensus of experts on a subject such as project risk.

B. It is a technique in which project risk experts participate anonymously.

C. It helps reduce bias in the data and keeps any one person from having undue influence on the outcome.

D. It is based on an ancient Greek technique to ensure that actions of subordinates are aligned with the vision of senior executives.

162. The risk rating:

A. Is calculated by multiplying the probability of the occurrence of a risk times its impact (relative scale) on an objective (e.g., cost, time, scope, or quality) if it were to occur.

B. Is the sum of squares of the scale values assigned to the estimates of probability and impact.

C. Cannot be used to determine whether a risk is considered low, moderate, or high.

D. Is a commonly used technique for risk avoidance.

163. Sensitivity analysis:

A. Examines the extent to which the uncertainty of project objectives affects each project element simultaneously.

B. Examines the extent to which the uncertainty of each project element affects the objective being examined when all other uncertain elements are held at their baseline values.

C. Is a method for assessing stakeholders' tolerance to risk.

D. Cannot be used to determine which risks have the most potential impact on the project.

164. All of the following are characteristics of a decision tree EXCEPT:

A. A decision tree is a diagram that describes a decision under consideration and the implications of choosing one or another of the available alternatives.

B. Decision tree analysis is a risk analysis tool that can be used to choose the most appropriate responses.

C. A decision tree is primarily a graphical, qualitative risk analysis technique and is not generally used in quantitative risk analysis.

D. Decision tree analysis uses expected monetary value (EMV) analysis to help the organization identify the relative values of alternative actions.

165. The risk management plan generally includes all of the following EXCEPT:

A. Methodology.

B. Definitions of risk probability and impact.

C. Responses to individual risks.

D. Probability and impact matrix.

166. The Perform Qualitative Risk Analysis process assesses the priority of identified risks using all of the following EXCEPT:

A. Relative probability or likelihood of occurrence of identified risks.

B. Impact on project objectives if the identified risks occur.

C. A mathematical technique, such as expected monetary value (EMV), to create the impression of precision and accuracy.

D. The organization's risk tolerance associated with the project constraints of cost, schedule, scope, and quality.

167. As an output of the Monitor and Control Risks process, an updated risk register generally includes some or all of the following EXCEPT:

A. The work breakdown structure (WBS).

B. Outcomes of risk reassessments, risk audits, and periodic risk reviews.

C. Identification of new risk events, updates to probability, impact, priority, response plans, ownership, and other elements of the risk register.

D. Outcomes of the project's risks and of the risk responses.

168. Expected monetary value (EMV) analysis has all of the following characteristics EXCEPT:

A. It is a statistical concept that calculates the average outcome when the future includes scenarios that may or may not happen.

B. The EMV of opportunities will generally be expressed as positive values, while those of risks will be negative.

C. EMV analysis cannot be used effectively in decision tree analysis unless a risk-averse assumption is made.

D. EMV is calculated by multiplying the value of each possible outcome by its probability of occurrence and adding the products together.

Project Procurement Management

(Chapter 12 of the *PMBOK® Guide*)

169. All of the following are inputs to the Plan Procurements process EXCEPT:

A. Scope baseline.

B. Risk register.

C. Application area extensions.

D. Enterprise environmental factors.

170. Generally, a bid differs from a proposal in that the term:

A. Proposal is used when source selection will be based on price.

B. Proposal is used when the project time frame is limited.

C. Bid is used when the seller selection decision will be based on price.

D. Bid is used when technical capability and technical approach considerations are paramount.

171. The buyer structures procurement documents to accomplish all of the following EXCEPT:

A. Facilitate an accurate and complete response from each prospective seller.

B. Include a description of the desired form of the response.

C. Include the relevant procurement statement of work (SOW) and any required contractual provisions.

D. Provide a list of potential bidders to each prospective seller.

172. Approved change requests can generally include all of the following EXCEPT:

A. Modifications to the terms and conditions of the contract.

B. Modification to pricing.

C. Seller invoices.

D. Modification to the description of the products, services, or results to be provided.

173. **Which of the following is false about advertising as one of the Conduct Procurements process tools and techniques?**

A. Some government jurisdictions require public advertising of certain types of procurement items.

B. Advertising can often be used to expand existing lists of potential sellers.

C. Advertising in general circulation publications can cause public pressure resulting in bid disputes.

D. Advertising can be placed in general circulation publications, such as selected newspapers, or in specialty trade publications.

174. **Payment systems generally include all of the following characteristics EXCEPT:**

A. Payments are typically processed after certification of satisfactory work by an authorized person on the project team.

B. All payments should be made and documented in strict accordance with the terms of the contract.

C. Renegotiations of price and other terms of the contract are typically conducted prior to authorizing payments to the seller.

D. Payments to the seller are typically processed by the accounts payable system of the buyer.

175. **The buyer, usually through its authorized procurement administrator, provides the seller with _____ as an output of the Close Procurements process.**

A. Formal written notice that the deliverables have been accepted or rejected.

B. Letters of commendation to all project team members.

C. Informal notice of acceptance of the deliverables.

D. A copy of the internal notice of completion provided to senior management.

176. **In which type of contract must buyers precisely specify the product or services being procured?**

A. Cost plus award fee contract.

B. Fixed-price contract.

C. Cost-reimbursable contract.

D. Partnership contract.

177. Which of the following is one of the terms used to describe contested changes and potential constructive changes where the buyer and seller cannot reach an agreement on compensation for the change, or cannot agree that a change has occurred?

A. Forcing.

B. Mediation.

C. Complaints.

D. Claims.

178. Constructive changes are:

A. Postponed as long as possible to protect the budget.

B. Viewed as negative, quantified, and tabulated.

C. Uniquely identified and documented by project correspondence.

D. Submitted for bids to the relevant vendor list.

179. The procurement audit has all of the following characteristics EXCEPT:

A. It maintains a complete file of procurement-related records.

B. It is a structured review of the procurement process.

C. It is a review of the procurement process originating from the Plan Procurements process through the Administer Procurements process.

D. Its objective is to identify successes and failures that warrant recognition.

180. Different types of contracts may be in the best interests of the project. Contracts generally fall into one of the following broad categories EXCEPT:

A. Request for proposal (RFP).

B. Fixed-price contracts.

C. Cost-reimbursable contracts.

D. Time and material contracts (T&M).

181. **All of the following are true about the statement of work (SOW) for a procurement EXCEPT:**

A. It describes the procurement item in sufficient detail to allow prospective sellers to determine if they are capable of providing the products, services, or results.

B. It should be as ambiguous, incomplete, and wordy as possible to allow for future negotiations.

C. It can include specifications, quantity desired, quality levels, performance data, period of performance, work location, and other requirements.

D. It can be revised and refined as required as it moves through the procurement process until incorporated into a signed contract award.

182. **Outputs from the Close Procurements process generally include all of the following EXCEPT:**

A. Closed procurements.

B. Formal written notice that the deliverables have been accepted or rejected.

C. The Request for Proposal (RFP) or Request for Quotation (RFQ), and the contractor's working proposal.

D. Lessons learned documentation.

183. Source selection criteria are developed and used to rate or score seller proposals. These criteria have generally all of the following characteristics EXCEPT:

A. They are often included as a part of the procurement solicitation documents.

B. They can be objective or subjective.

C. They can be limited to the purchase price if the procurement item is readily available from a number of acceptable sellers.

D. They generally require specification of the name of the transportation organization responsible for delivery of procured products.

184. All of the following are tools and techniques of the Conduct Procurements process EXCEPT:

A. Proposal evaluation techniques.

B. Independent estimates.

C. Procurement negotiations.

D. Resource distribution system.

185. Cost-plus-fixed-fee contracts (CPFF) have all of the following characteristics EXCEPT:

A. Seller is reimbursed for all allowable costs for performing the contract work.

B. Seller receives a fixed fee payment calculated as a percentage of the actual project costs.

C. Seller receives a fixed fee payment calculated as a percentage of the initial estimated project costs.

D. The fixed fee does not change due to seller performance unless the project scope changes.

Glossary

186. Acceptance Criteria:

A. Are developed during phase-end reviews to ensure authorization to close the current phase and start the subsequent one.

B. Must be met before project deliverables are accepted.

C. Can be passive or active allowing the project team to deal with the risks as they occur.

D. Are distinct from performance requirements in that acceptance criteria are aimed at meeting or exceeding technical specifications.

187. The baseline is the approved:

A. Project schedule and budget.

B. Description in the project charter.

C. Plan for a project, plus or minus approved changes.

D. Starting point for contract negotiations.

188. A code of accounts:

A. Is any numbering system used to uniquely identify each component of the work breakdown structure.

B. Includes work packages, used to track phase completion.

C. Is an organizational scheme to keep track of contracts.

D. Charts elements of the WBS against the timeline.

189. A stakeholder is a(n):

A. Project engineer.

B. Individual or agency that controls contingency funds and their disbursement through the project management office (PMO).

C. Organization's corporate attorney.

D. Person or organization that is actively involved in the project, or whose interests may be positively or negatively affected by execution or completion of the project.

190. The scope management plan for a project is:

A. The project specifications that include project objectives, design principles, and guidance on how the project will be controlled.

B. A three-level project work breakdown structure that shows how project scope will be managed.

C. The document that describes how the project scope will be defined, developed, and verified.

D. The document that shows that all project deliverables were completed satisfactorily.

191. The project scope statement:

A. Provides a documented basis for making future project decisions and for confirming or developing a common understanding of project scope among the stakeholders.

B. Determines the boundary conditions and responses required to perform project activities.

C. Is a narrative analysis of project activities, activity sequences, activity durations, and resource requirements.

D. Is a written statement that identifies the quality standards relevant to project deliverables and describes how to achieve those standards.

192. A work package is:

A. A summary task or a hammock activity at the top level of the work breakdown structure (WBS).

B. A deliverable or project work component at the lowest level of each branch of the work breakdown structure (WBS).

C. A management control point that may include one or more control accounts to plan a project deliverable and establish integrated schedule change control.

D. A milestone required for completion of a project deliverable in the work breakdown structure (WBS) or a work activity on the critical path.

193. In what way does free float differ from total float?

A. Free float is the amount of total float that does not affect the schedule end date, whereas total float is the total accumulated amount of free float.

B. There is no difference—the two terms are functionally equivalent and are used in different application areas.

C. Free float is the amount of time that a schedule activity can be delayed without delaying the early start date of any immediately following schedule activities, whereas total float is the total amount of time that a schedule activity may be delayed from its early start date without delaying the project finish date, or violating a schedule constraint.

D. Free float of a schedule activity is calculated by subtracting the total float of the schedule activity from the total float of the critical path, without violating other schedule constraints.

194. The project's performance measurement baseline:

A. Is used to measure and manage performance.

B. Changes frequently.

C. Documents relevant performance standards of the project team.

D. Can be generally changed by the project team to reflect adherence to project objectives.

195. What does cost of quality mean?

A. The sacrifice of unessential project objectives to meet essential quality standards.

B. The life cycle cost of the project, including costs for quality planning and failure costs.

C. Determining the costs incurred to ensure quality.

D. Determining the costs of meeting project objectives, including costs for quality control, quality assurance, and rework.

196. FFP is an acronym for:

A. Free-Flow Performance.

B. Firm-Fixed-Price.

C. Free-Form Project.

D. Fixed-File Procurement.

197. The approved project baseline should be changed:

A. When a sequence of activities has taken longer than originally planned or cost more than originally estimated, and in excess of the thresholds established in the performance management plan.

B. When a change request is generated and approved through the Perform Integrated Change Control process.

C. When the productivity within a certain discipline has been higher or lower than originally planned, and in excess of the thresholds established in the performance measurement plan.

D. When a high-duration activity has been accomplished "out-of-sequence."

198. All of the following are true about the product life cycle EXCEPT:

A. It is a collection of generally sequential, non-overlapping product phases.

B. The last product life cycle phase for a product is generally the product's retirement.

C. Generally, a project life cycle is contained within one or more product life cycles.

D. Generally, a project life cycle contains one or more product life cycles.

199. The performance measurement baseline:

A. Typically covers the schedule, and may include cost parameters of a project, but does not include technical and quality parameters.

B. Changes periodically to accommodate current performance information about the project.

C. Is the approved integrated scope-schedule-cost plan for the project work against which project execution is compared, and may include technical and quality parameters.

D. Is generally revised at regular project review meetings to manage stakeholder expectations.

200. Workaround is:

A. A response to a negative risk that has occurred. A workaround is not planned in advance of the occurrence of the risk event.

B. A contingency plan to avoid, transfer, or mitigate a negative risk or threat.

C. Implementation of the established contingency plan to avoid a negative risk or threat, or to exploit a positive risk or an opportunity.

D. Using global sourcing to continue project work around the clock.

Appendix G
(Interpersonal Skills)

201. All of the following are generally true about leadership in a project environment EXCEPT:

A. It involves focusing the efforts of a group of people toward a common goal and enabling them to work as a team.

B. It is the ability to get things done through others.

C. Respect and trust, rather than fear and submission, are the key elements of effective leadership.

D. Although important throughout all project phases, effective leadership is critical during the closing phase when the emphasis is on stakeholder acceptance of the project.

202. Team building has all of the following characteristics EXCEPT:

A. It is the process of helping a group of individuals, bound by a common sense of purpose, to work interdependently with each other, the leader, external stakeholders, and the organization.

B. It requires handling project team problems decisively and removing the individual responsible for these problems from the team promptly to ensure a productive, smooth project environment.

C. It can be enhanced by obtaining top management support, encouraging team member commitment, introducing appropriate rewards, recognition, and ethics.

D. It can be enhanced by creating a team identity, managing conflicts effectively, promoting trust and open communication among team members, and providing leadership.

203. Motivating involves creating an environment to meet project objectives while offering maximum self-satisfaction related to what people value most. These values generally include all of the following EXCEPT:

A. A sense of accomplishment, achievement, and growth.

B. Sufficient financial compensation.

C. Accurate criticism in the annual performance review or after the project is completed.

D. Opportunity to apply one's professional skills to meet new challenges at work.

204. Project managers spend the majority of their time communicating with team members and other project stakeholders. To communicate effectively, the project manager should generally do all of the following EXCEPT:

A. Calculate the potential number of communication channels accurately and update it regularly to develop a bridge between diverse stakeholders and a common perspective on the project among them, regardless of their cultural and organizational backgrounds.

B. Develop an awareness of the communication styles of other parties involved in the project.

C. Develop an awareness of cultural issues, relationships, and personalities of project stakeholders.

D. Understand what information to provide, what information to receive, and which interpersonal skills will help communicate effectively with various project stakeholders.

205. Cultural differences:

A. Are primarily individual issues that need to be avoided in project teams.

B. Involve internal stakeholders primarily and should not be apparent to external stakeholders because such differences do not involve them.

C. Can impact the speed of working, the decision-making process, and the impulse to act without appropriate planning.

D. Should not generally lead to conflict and stress in organizations. Therefore, they do not affect the performance of professionals working on project teams and their ability to meet project objectives.

Q & As
FOR THE
PMBOK® GUIDE
FOURTH EDITION
Answers

Introduction
(Chapter 1 of the *PMBOK® Guide*)

1. Answer: D.
PMBOK® Guide, page 5, Section 1.2

What is a project?
A project is a temporary endeavor undertaken to create a unique product, service, or result.

2. Answer: B.
PMBOK® Guide, page 6, Section 1.3

What is project management?
Project management is the application of knowledge, skills, tools, and techniques to project activities to meet project requirements.

3. Answer: A.
PMBOK® Guide, pages 6–7, Section 1.3

Managing a project typically includes:
- Identifying requirements,
- Addressing the various needs, concerns, and expectations of the stakeholders as the project is planned and carried out,
- Balancing the competing project constraints including, but not limited to:
  - Scope,
  - Quality,
  - Schedule,
  - Budget,
  - Resources, and
  - Risk.

The specific project will influence the constraints on which the project manager needs to focus.

4. Answer: C.
PMBOK® Guide, pages 8–9, Section 1.4.1

Portfolio Management
Portfolio management refers to the centralized management of one or more portfolios, which includes identifying, prioritizing, authorizing, managing, and controlling projects, programs, and other related work, to achieve specific strategic business objectives. Portfolio management focuses on ensuring that projects and programs are reviewed to prioritize resource allocation, and that the management of the portfolio is consistent with and aligned to organizational strategies.

5. Answer: C.

PMBOK® Guide, pages 8–9, Section 1.4.1, Table 1-1

Comparative Overview of Project, Program, and Portfolio Management

As shown in Table 1-1, under the heading *Projects*:
Success is measured by product and project quality, timeliness, budget compliance, and degree of customer satisfaction.

6. Answer: B.

PMBOK® Guide, page 9, Section 1.4.2

Program Management

A program is defined as a group of related projects managed in a coordinated way to obtain benefits and control not available from managing them individually. Programs may include elements of related work outside the scope of the discrete projects in the program. A project may or may not be part of a program but a program will always have projects.

7. Answer: A.
PMBOK® Guide, pages 11–12, Section 1.4.4

Project Management Office
A project management office (PMO) is an organizational body or entity assigned various responsibilities related to the centralized and coordinated management of those projects under its domain. The responsibilities of a PMO can range from providing project management support functions to actually being responsible for the direct management of a project.

The projects supported or administered by the PMO may not be related, other than by being managed together. The specific form, function, and structure of a PMO are dependent upon the needs of the organization that it supports.

A PMO may be delegated the authority to act as an integral stakeholder and a key decision maker during the beginning of each project, to make recommendations or to terminate projects or to take other actions as required to keep business objectives consistent. In addition, the PMO may be involved in the selection, management, and deployment of shared or dedicated project resources.

A primary function of a PMO is to support project managers in a variety of ways which may include, but are not limited to:
- Managing shared resources across all projects administered by the PMO;
- Identifying and developing project management methodology, best practices, and standards;
- Coaching, mentoring, training, and oversight;
- Monitoring compliance with project management standards, policies, procedures, and templates via project audits;

- Developing and managing project policies, procedures, templates, and other shared documentation (organizational process assets); and
- Coordinating communication across projects.

Project managers and PMOs pursue different objectives and, as such, are driven by different requirements. All of these efforts, however, are aligned with the strategic needs of the organization. Differences between the role of project managers and a PMO may include the following:

- The project manager focuses on the specified project objectives, while the PMO manages major program scope changes which may be seen as potential opportunities to better achieve business objectives.
- The project manager controls the assigned project resources to best meet project objectives, while the PMO optimizes the use of shared organizational resources across all projects.
- The project manager manages the constraints (scope, schedule, cost, and quality, etc.) of the individual projects while the PMO manages the methodologies, standards, overall risk/opportunity, and interdependencies among projects at the enterprise level.

8. Answer: D.
PMBOK® Guide, page 12, Section 1.5

Project Management and Operations Management
Operations are an organizational function performing the ongoing execution of activities that produce the same product or provide a repetitive service. Examples include: production operations, manufacturing operations, and accounting operations. Though temporary in nature, projects can help achieve the organizational goals when they are aligned with the organization's strategy. Organizations sometimes change their operations, products, or systems by creating strategic business initiatives. Projects require project management while operations require business process management or operations management. Projects can intersect with operations at various points during the product life cycle, such as:
* At each closeout phase;
* When developing a new product, upgrading a product, or expanding outputs;
* Improvement of operations or the product development process; or
* Until the divestment of the operations at the end of the product life cycle.

At each point, deliverables and knowledge are transferred between the project and operations for implementation of the delivered work. This occurs through a transfer of project resources to operations toward the end of the project, or through a transfer of operational resources to the project at the start.

Operations are permanent endeavors that produce repetitive outputs, with resources assigned to do basically the same set of tasks according to the standards institutionalized in a product life cycle. Unlike the ongoing nature of operations, projects are temporary endeavors.

9. Answer: C.
PMBOK® Guide, pages 13–14, Section 1.7

Project Management Body of Knowledge
The *PMBOK® Guide* is the standard for managing most projects most of the time across many types of industries. This standard describes the project management processes, tools, and techniques used to manage a project toward a successful outcome.

This standard is unique to the project management field and has interrelationships to other project management disciplines such as program management and portfolio management.

Project management standards do not address all details of every topic. This standard is limited to single projects and the project management processes that are generally recognized as good practice. Other standards may be consulted for additional information on the broader context in which projects are accomplished. Management of programs is addressed in *The Standard for Program Management* – Second Edition, and management of portfolios is addressed in *The Standard for Portfolio Management* – Second Edition. Examination of an enterprise's project management process capabilities is addressed in *Organizational Project Management Maturity Model (OPM3®)* – Second Edition.

10. Answer: D.
PMBOK® Guide, page 14, Section 1.8

Enterprise Environmental Factors
Enterprise environmental factors refer to both internal and external environmental factors that surround or influence a project's success. These factors may come from any or all of the enterprises involved in the project. Enterprise environmental factors may enhance or constrain project management options and may have a positive or negative influence on the outcome. They are considered as inputs to most planning processes.

Enterprise environmental factors include, but are not limited to:
- Organizational culture, structure, and processes;
- Government or industry standards (e.g., regulatory agency regulations, codes of conduct, product standards, quality standards, and workmanship standards);
- Infrastructure (e.g., existing facilities and capital equipment);
- Existing human resources (e.g., skills, disciplines, and knowledge, such as design, development, law, contracting, and purchasing);
- Personnel administration (e.g., staffing and retention guidelines, employee performance reviews and training records, overtime policy, and time tracking);
- Company work authorization systems;
- Marketplace conditions;
- Stakeholder risk tolerances;
- Political climate;
- Organization's established communications channels;
- Commercial databases (e.g., standardized cost estimating data, industry risk study information, and risk databases); and
- Project management information systems (e.g., an automated tool, such as a scheduling software tool, a configuration management system, an information collection and distribution system, or web interfaces to other online automated systems).

Project Life Cycle and Organization
(Chapter 2 of the *PMBOK® Guide*)

11. Answer: B.
PMBOK® Guide, page 15, Section 2.1

The Project Life Cycle—Overview
A project life cycle is a collection of generally
sequential and sometimes overlapping project phases
whose name and number are determined by the
management and control needs of the organization or
organizations involved in the project, the nature of the
project itself, and its area of application. A life cycle
can be documented with a methodology. The project
life cycle can be determined or shaped by the unique
aspects of the organization, industry or technology
employed. While every project has a definite start and
a definite end, the specific deliverables and activities
that take place in between will vary widely with the
project. The life cycle provides the basic framework for
managing the project, regardless of the specific work
involved.

12. Answer: D.

PMBOK® Guide, pages 16–17, Section 2.1.1, Figure 2-1, and Figure 2-2

Characteristics of the Project Life Cycle
The generic life cycle structure generally displays the following characteristics:
- Cost and staffing levels are low at the start, peak as the work is carried out, and drop rapidly as the project draws to a close. The dashed line in Figure 2-1 illustrates this typical pattern.
- Stakeholder influences, risk, and uncertainty, (as illustrated in Figure 2-2) are greatest at the start of the project. These factors decrease over the life of the project.
- Ability to influence the final characteristics of the project's product, without significantly impacting cost, is highest at the start of the project and decreases as the project progresses towards completion. Figure 2-2 illustrates the idea that the cost of changes and correcting errors typically increases substantially as the project approaches completion.

13. Answer: A.

PMBOK® Guide, page 23, Section 2.3

Stakeholders
Stakeholders are persons or organizations (e.g., customers, sponsors, the performing organization, or the public), who are actively involved in the project or whose interests may be positively or negatively affected by the performance or completion of the project. Stakeholders may also exert influence over the project, its deliverables, and the project team members.

14. Answer: C.
PMBOK® Guide, page 23, Section 2.3

Stakeholders
The project management team must identify both internal and external stakeholders in order to determine the project requirements and expectations of all parties involved. Furthermore, the project manager must manage the influence of the various stakeholders in relation to the project requirements to ensure a successful outcome.

15. Answer: D.
PMBOK® Guide, page 27, Section 2.4.1

Organizational Cultures and Styles
Cultures and styles may have a strong influence on a project's ability to meet its objectives. Cultures and styles are typically known as "cultural norms." The "norms" include a common knowledge regarding how to approach getting the work done, what means are considered acceptable for getting the work done, and who is influential in facilitating the work getting done.

Most organizations have developed unique cultures that manifest in numerous ways. . .

16. Answer: C.
PMBOK® Guide, pages 28–30, Section 2.4.2 and Table 2-1; and page 31, Figure 2-11

Organizational Structure
At the opposite end of the spectrum to the functional organization is the projectized organization, shown in Figure 2-11. In a projectized organization, team members are often co-located, most of the organization's resources are involved in project work, and project managers have a great deal of independence and authority. Projectized organizations often have organizational units called departments, but these groups either report directly to the project manager or provide support services to the various projects.

17. Answer: A.
PMBOK® Guide, pages 28–30, Section 2.4.2 and Table 2-1; and page 29, Figure 2-7

Organizational Structure
Organizational structure is an enterprise environmental factor which can affect the availability of resources and influence how projects are conducted. Organizational structures range from functional to projectized, with a variety of matrix structures between them. Table 2-1 shows key project-related characteristics of the major types of organizational structures.

The classic functional organization, shown in Figure 2-7, is a hierarchy where each employee has one clear superior. Staff members are grouped by specialty, such as production, marketing, engineering, and accounting at the top level. Specialties may be further subdivided into functional organizations, such as mechanical and electrical engineering. Each department in a functional organization will do its project work independent of other departments.

18. Answer: C.
PMBOK® Guide, pages 28–29, Section 2.4.2 and Figure 2-8

Organizational Structure
Matrix organizations, as shown in Figures 2-8 through 2-10, are a blend of functional and projectized characteristics. Weak matrices maintain many of the characteristics of a functional organization, and the project manager role is more of a coordinator or expediter than that of a true project manager. Strong matrices have many of the characteristics of the projectized organization, and can have full-time project managers with considerable authority and full-time project administrative staff. While the balanced matrix organization recognizes the need for a project manager, it does not provide the project manager with the full authority over the project and project funding.

19. Answer: C.
PMBOK® Guide, page 28, Section 2.4.2 and Table 2-1

Organizational Structure
Organizational structure is an enterprise environmental factor which can affect the availability of resources and influence how projects are conducted. Organizational structures range from functional to projectized, with a variety of matrix structures between them. Table 2-1 shows key project-related characteristics of the major types of organizational structures.

20. Answer: A.

PMBOK® Guide, pages 28–30, Section 2.4.2 and Table 2-1; and page 31, Figure 2-11

Organizational Structure

Organizational structure is an enterprise environmental factor which can affect the availability of resources and influence how projects are conducted. Organizational structures range from functional to projectized, with a variety of matrix structures between them. Table 2-1 shows key project-related characteristics of the major types of organizational structures.

At the opposite end of the spectrum to the functional organization is the projectized organization, shown in Figure 2-11. In a projectized organization, team members are often co-located, most of the organization's resources are involved in project work, and project managers have a great deal of independence and authority. Projectized organizations often have organizational units called departments, but these groups either report directly to the project manager or provide support services to the various projects.

21. Answer: B.
PMBOK® Guide, pages 23–26, Section 2.3 and Figure 2-6

Stakeholders
- Project management office. A project management office (PMO) is an organizational body or entity assigned various responsibilities related to the centralized and coordinated management of those projects under its domain. The responsibilities of a PMO can range from providing project management support functions to actually being responsible for the direct management of a project. The PMO can be a stakeholder if it has direct or indirect responsibility for the outcome of the project. The PMO can provide but is not limited to:
  - Administrative support services such as policies, methodologies, and templates;
  - Training, mentoring, and coaching of project managers;
  - Project support, guidance, and training on how to manage projects and the use of tools;
  - Resource alignment of project staff; and/or
  - Centralized communication among project managers, project sponsors, managers, and other stakeholders.

22. Answer: C.

PMBOK® Guide, pages 23–24, Section 2.3

Stakeholders

A project can be perceived as having both positive and negative results by the stakeholders. Some stakeholders benefit from a successful project, while other stakeholders perceive negative outcomes from a project's success, for example, business leaders from a community that will benefit from an industrial expansion project by positive economic benefits to the community. In the case of stakeholders with positive expectations from the project, their interests are best served by helping the project succeed. The interests of negative stakeholders are served by impeding the project's progress. Overlooking negative stakeholders can result in an increased likelihood of failure. An important part of a project manager's responsibility is to manage stakeholder expectations. This can be difficult because stakeholders often have very different or conflicting objectives. Part of the project manager's responsibility is to balance these interests and ensure that the project team interacts with stakeholders in a professional and cooperative manner.

23. Answer: A.

PMBOK® Guide, pages 28–30, Section 2.4.2 and Table 2-1; and page 30, Figure 2-10

Organizational Structure

Strong matrices have many of the characteristics of the projectized organization, and can have full-time project managers with considerable authority and full-time project administrative staff. While the balanced matrix organization recognizes the need for a project manager, it does not provide the project manager with the full authority over the project and project funding. Table 2-1 provides additional details of the various matrix organizational structures.

24. Answer: D.
PMBOK® Guide, pages 28–29, Section 2.4.2 and Table 2-1

Organizational Structure
Weak matrices maintain many of the characteristics of a functional organization, and the project manager role is more of a coordinator or expediter than that of a true project manager. Strong matrices have many of the characteristics of the projectized organization, and can have full-time project managers with considerable authority and full-time project administrative staff. While the balanced matrix organization recognizes the need for a project manager, it does not provide the project manager with the full authority over the project and project funding. Table 2-1 provides additional details of the various matrix organizational structures.

25. Answer: C.

PMBOK® Guide, page 18, Section 2.1.2; and Glossary

Product vs. Project Life Cycle Relationships
The product life cycle consists of generally sequential, non-overlapping product phases determined by the manufacturing and control need of the organization. The last product life cycle phase for a product is generally the product's retirement. Project life cycles occur in one or more phases of a product life cycle. Care should be taken to distinguish the project life cycle from the product life cycle. All projects have a purpose or objective, but in those cases where the objective is a service or result, there may be a life cycle for the service or result, not a product life cycle.

Product Life Cycle. A collection of generally sequential, non-overlapping product phases whose name and number are determined by the manufacturing and control needs of the organization. The last product life cycle phase for a product is generally the product's retirement. Generally, a project life cycle is contained within one or more product life cycles.

Project Life Cycle. A collection of generally sequential project phases whose name and number are determined by the control needs of the organization or organizations involved in the project. A life cycle can be documented with a methodology.

Project Management Processes for a Project

(Chapter 3 of the *PMBOK® Guide*)

26. Answer: B.

PMBOK® Guide, pages 38–39, Introduction

Project management processes are grouped into five categories known as Project Management Process Groups (or Process Groups):

- **Initiating Process Group.** Those processes performed to define a new project or a new phase of an existing project by obtaining authorization to start the project or phase.
- **Planning Process Group.** Those processes required to establish the scope of the project, refine the objectives, and define the course of action required to attain the objectives that the project was undertaken to achieve.
- **Executing Process Group.** Those processes performed to complete the work defined in the project management plan to satisfy the project specifications.
- **Monitoring and Controlling Process Group.** Those processes required to track, review, and regulate the progress and performance of the project; identify any areas in which changes to the plan are required; and initiate the corresponding changes.
- **Closing Process Group.** Those processes performed to finalize all activities across all Process Groups to formally close the project or phase.

27. Answer: A.
PMBOK® Guide, page 40, Section 3.1; and page 41, Figure 3-2

Common Project Management Process Interactions
Project Management Process Groups are linked by the outputs they produce. The Process Groups are seldom either discrete or one-time events; they are overlapping activities that occur throughout the project. The output of one process generally becomes an input to another process or is a deliverable of the project. The Planning Process Group provides the Executing Process Group with the project management plan and project documents, and, as the project progresses, it often entails updates to the project management plan and the project documents. Figure 3-2 illustrates how the Process Groups interact and shows the level of overlap at various times. If the project is divided into phases, the Process Groups interact within each phase.

28. Answer: C.
PMBOK® Guide, page 40, Section 3.1

Common Project Management Process Interactions
Project Management Process Groups are linked by the outputs they produce. The Process Groups are seldom either discrete or one-time events; they are overlapping activities that occur throughout the project. The output of one process generally becomes an input to another process or is a deliverable of the project.

29. Answer: D.
PMBOK® Guide, pages 40–41, Sections 3.1 and 3.2

Common Project Management Process Interactions
If the project is divided into phases, the Process Groups interact within each phase.

Project Management Process Groups
The Process Groups are not project phases. When large or complex projects are separated into distinct phases or subprojects such as feasibility study, concept development, design, prototype, build, test, etc., all of the Process Groups would normally be repeated for each phase or subproject.

30. Answer: C.
PMBOK® Guide, pages 37–38, Introduction

Project Management Processes for a Project
In order for a project to be successful, the project team must:
- Select appropriate processes required to meet the project objectives,
- Use a defined approach that can be adopted to meet requirements,
- Comply with requirements to meet stakeholder needs and expectations, and
- Balance the competing demands of scope, time, cost, quality, resources, and risk to produce the specified product, service, or result.

Project management processes apply globally and across industry groups. Good practice means there is general agreement that the application of project management processes has been shown to enhance the chances of success over a wide range of projects.

This does not mean that the knowledge, skills, and processes described should always be applied uniformly on all projects. For any given project, the project manager, in collaboration with the project team, is always responsible for determining which processes are appropriate, and the appropriate degree of rigor for each process.

31. Answer: C.
PMBOK® Guide, pages 39–41, Section 3.1, and Figures 3-1 and 3-2

Common Project Management Process Interactions
Project Management Process Groups are linked by the outputs they produce. The Process Groups are seldom either discrete or one-time events; they are overlapping activities that occur throughout the project. The output of one process generally becomes an input to another process or is a deliverable of the project. The Planning Process Group provides the Executing Process Group with the project management plan and project documents, and, as the project progresses, it often entails updates to the project management plan and the project documents. Figure 3-2 illustrates how the Process Groups interact and shows the level of overlap at various times. If the project is divided into phases, the Process Groups interact within each phase.

When a project is divided into phases, the Process Groups are invoked as appropriate to effectively drive the project to completion in a controlled manner. In multi-phase projects, processes are repeated within each phase until the criteria for phase completion have been satisfied.

32. Answer: A.
PMBOK® Guide, page 44, Section 3.3 and Figure 3-4

Initiating Process Group
The Initiating Process Group consists of those processes performed to define a new project or a new phase of an existing project by obtaining authorization to start the project or phase. Within the Initiating processes, the initial scope is defined and initial financial resources are committed. Internal and external stakeholders who will interact and influence the overall outcome of the project are identified. If not already assigned, the project manager will be selected. This information is captured in the project charter and stakeholder register. When the project charter is approved, the project becomes officially authorized. Although the project management team may help write the project charter, approval and funding are handled external to the project boundaries (Figure 3-4).

33. Answer: B.
PMBOK® Guide, page 44, Section 3.3

Initiating Process Group
Invoking the Initiating processes at the start of each phase helps keep the project focused on the business need the project was undertaken to address. The success criteria are verified, and the influence and objectives of the project stakeholders are reviewed. A decision is then made as to whether the project should be continued, delayed, or discontinued.

Involving the customers and other stakeholders during initiation generally improves the probability of shared ownership, deliverable acceptance, and customer and other stakeholder satisfaction.

34. Answer: B.
PMBOK® Guide, pages 46–48, Section 3.4; and page 52, Section 3.4.12

Planning Process Group
The Planning Process Group consists of those processes performed to establish the total scope of the effort, define and refine the objectives, and develop the course of action required to attain those objectives. The planning processes develop the project management plan and the project documents that will be used to carry out the project. . .

The Planning Process Group (Figure 3-8) includes the project management processes identified in Figures 3-9 through 3-28 (see Sections 3.4.1 through 3.4.20).

Plan Quality
Plan Quality is the process of identifying quality requirements and/or standards for the project and product, and documenting how the project will demonstrate compliance.

35. Answer: B.
PMBOK® Guide, page 59, Section 3.6; and page 62, Section 3.6.5

Monitoring and Controlling Process Group
The Monitoring and Controlling Process Group consists of those processes required to track, review, and regulate the progress and performance of the project; identify any areas in which changes to the plan are required; and initiate the corresponding changes.

Control Schedule
Control Schedule is the process of monitoring the status of the project to update project progress and managing changes to the schedule baseline.

36. Answer: D.

PMBOK® Guide, pages 55–56, Section 3.5 and Figure 3-29; and pages 64–65, Section 3.7

Executing Process Group

The Executing Process Group consists of those processes performed to complete the work defined in the project management plan to satisfy the project specifications. This Process Group involves coordinating people and resources, as well as integrating and performing the activities of the project in accordance with the project management plan (Figure 3-29).

Closing Process Group

The Closing Process Group consists of those processes performed to finalize all activities across all Project Management Process Groups to formally complete the project, phase, or contractual obligations.

Project Integration Management
(Chapter 4 of the *PMBOK® Guide*)

37. Answer: A.
PMBOK® Guide, page 71, Introduction; and page 73, Figure 4-1

Project Integration Management
Project Integration Management includes the processes and activities needed to identify, define, combine, unify, and coordinate the various processes and project management activities within the Project Management Process Groups. In the project management context, integration includes characteristics of unification, consolidation, articulation, and integrative actions that are crucial to project completion, successfully managing stakeholder expectations, and meeting requirements. . .

Figure 4-1 provides an overview of Project Integration Management processes, which are as follows:
4.1 Develop Project Charter
4.2 Develop Project Management Plan
4.3 Direct and Manage Project Execution
4.4 Monitor and Control Project Work
4.5 Perform Integrated Change Control
4.6 Close Project or Phase

38. Answer: C.
PMBOK® Guide, pages 73–74, Section 4.1

Develop Project Charter
Develop Project Charter is the process of developing a document that formally authorizes a project or a phase and documenting initial requirements that satisfy the stakeholders' needs and expectations. It establishes a partnership between the performing organization and the requesting organization (or customer, in the case of external projects). The approved project charter formally initiates the project. A project manager is identified and assigned as early in the project as is feasible, preferably while the project charter is being developed and always prior to the start of planning. It is recommended that the project manager participate in the development of the project charter, as the project charter provides the project manager with the authority to apply resources to project activities.

Projects are authorized by someone external to the project such as a sponsor, PMO, or portfolio steering committee. The project initiator or sponsor should be at a level that is appropriate to funding the project. They will either create the project charter or delegate that duty to the project manager. The initiator's signature on the charter authorizes the project. Projects are authorized due to internal business needs or external influences. This usually triggers the creation of a needs analysis, business case, or description of the situation the project will address. Chartering a project links the project to the strategy and ongoing work of the organization.

39. Answer: D.

PMBOK® Guide page 95, Figure 4-10; and page 98, Section 4.5.2

Perform Integrated Change Control: Tools and Techniques
.1 Expert Judgment
In addition to the project management team's expert judgment, stakeholders may be asked to provide their expertise and may be asked to sit on the change control board. . .
.2 Change Control Meetings
A change control board is responsible for meeting and reviewing the change requests and approving or rejecting those change requests. . .

40. Answer: A.

PMBOK® Guide page 93, Section 4.5

Perform Integrated Change Control
Perform Integrated Change Control is the process of reviewing all change requests, approving changes and managing changes to the deliverables, organizational process assets, project documents and the project management plan. The Perform Integrated Change Control process is conducted from project inception through completion. The project management plan, the project scope statement, and other deliverables are maintained by carefully and continuously managing changes, either by rejecting changes or by approving changes thereby assuring that only approved changes are incorporated into a revised baseline.

The Perform Integrated Change Control process includes the following change management activities in differing levels of detail, based upon the progress of project execution:
• Maintaining the integrity of baselines by releasing only approved changes for incorporation into the project management plan and project documents.

41. Answer: B.

PMBOK® Guide, page 94, Section 4.5

Perform Integrated Change Control

A configuration management system with integrated change control provides a standardized, effective, and efficient way to centrally manage approved changes and baselines within a project. Configuration control is focused on the specification of both the deliverables and the processes while change control is focused on identifying, documenting, and controlling changes to the project and the product baselines

42. Answer: C.

PMBOK® Guide page 94, Section 4.5; and Glossary

Perform Integrated Change Control

Every documented change request must be either approved or rejected by some authority within the project management team or an external organization. On many projects, the project manager is given authority to approve certain types of change requests as defined in the project's roles and responsibilities documentation. Whenever required, the Perform Integrated Change Control process includes a change control board (CCB) responsible for approving or rejecting change requests. The roles and responsibilities of these boards are clearly defined within the configuration control and change control procedures, and are agreed upon by appropriate stakeholders. Many large organizations provide for a multi-tiered board structure, separating responsibilities among the boards. If the project is being provided under a contract, then some proposed changes may need to be approved by the customer as per the contract.

Change Control Board (CCB). A formally constituted group of stakeholders responsible for reviewing, evaluating, approving, delaying, or rejecting changes to a project, with all decisions and recommendations being recorded.

43. Answer: B.
PMBOK® Guide, page 93, Section 4.5

Perform Integrated Change Control
The Perform Integrated Change Control process
includes the following change management activities in
differing levels of detail, based upon the progress of
project execution:
- Influencing the factors that circumvent integrated
  change control so that only approved changes are
  implemented;
- Reviewing, analyzing, and approving change
  requests promptly, which is essential, as a slow
  decision may negatively affect time, cost, or the
  feasibility of a change;
- Managing the approved changes;
- Maintaining the integrity of baselines by releasing
  only approved changes for incorporation into the
  project management plan and project documents;
- Reviewing, approving, or denying all recommended
  corrective and preventive actions;
- Coordinating changes across the entire project (e.g.,
  a proposed schedule change will often affect cost,
  risk, quality, and staffing); and
- Documenting the complete impact of change
  requests.

44. Answer: D.
PMBOK® Guide, page 87, Section 4.3.2

**Direct and Manage Project Execution: Tools and
Techniques**
.2 Project Management Information System
The project management information system, part of
the enterprise environmental factors, provides access to
an automated tool, such as a scheduling software tool,
a configuration management system, an information
collection and distribution system, or web interfaces to
other online automated systems used during the Direct
and Manage Project Execution effort.

45. Answer: D.
PMBOK® Guide, pages 92–93, Section 4.4.3; and page 101–102, Section 4.6.3

> **Monitor and Control Project Work: Outputs**
> **.1 Change Requests**
> **.2 Project Management Plan Updates**
> **.3 Project Document Updates**
>
> **Close Project or Phase: Outputs**
> **.1 Final Product, Service, or Result Transition**
> **.2 Organizational Process Assets Updates**

46. Answer: A.
PMBOK® Guide, pages 99–100, Section 4.6

> **Close Project or Phase**
> Close Project or Phase is the process of finalizing all activities across all of the Project Management Process Groups to formally complete the project or phase.
>
> This includes all of the activities necessary for administrative closure of the project or phase, including step-by-step methodologies that address:
> * Actions and activities necessary to satisfy completion or exit criteria for the phase or project;
> * Actions and activities necessary to transfer the project's products, services, or results to the next phase or to production and/or operations; and
> * Activities needed to collect project or phase records, audit project success or failure, gather lessons learned and archive project information for future use by the organization.

Project Scope Management
(Chapter 5 of the *PMBOK® Guide*)

47. Answer: D.
PMBOK® Guide, page 104, Introduction; and page 126, Section 5.5.1.1

Project Scope Management
Although not shown here as a discrete process, the work involved in performing the five processes of Project Scope Management is preceded by a planning effort by the project management team. This planning effort is part of the Develop Project Management Plan process (Section 4.2), which produces a scope management plan that provides guidance on how project scope will be defined, documented, verified, managed, and controlled. The scope management plan may be formal or informal, highly detailed, or broadly framed, based upon the needs of the project.

Project Management Plan
The project management plan described in Section 4.2.3.1 contains the following information that is used to control scope:
- **Scope management plan**. The scope management plan describes how the project scope will be managed and controlled.

48. Answer: D.
PMBOK® Guide, page 105, Section 5.1

Collect Requirements
Collect Requirements is the process of defining and documenting stakeholders' needs to meet the project objectives. The project's success is directly influenced by the care taken in capturing and managing project and product requirements. Requirements include the quantified and documented needs and expectations of the sponsor, customer, and other stakeholders. These requirements need to be elicited, analyzed, and recorded in enough detail to be measured once project execution begins. Collecting requirements is defining and managing customer expectations. Requirements become the foundation of the WBS. Cost, schedule, and quality planning are all built upon these requirements. The development of requirements begins with an analysis of the information contained in the project charter (Section 4.1.3.1) and the stakeholder register (Section 10.1.3.1).

49. Answer: A.
PMBOK® Guide, page 115, Section 5.2.3.1

Project Scope Statement
The project scope statement describes, in detail, the project's deliverables and the work required to create those deliverables. The project scope statement also provides a common understanding of the project scope among project stakeholders. It may contain explicit scope exclusions that can assist in managing stakeholder expectations. It enables the project team to perform more detailed planning, guides the project team's work during execution, and provides the baseline for evaluating whether requests for changes or additional work are contained within or outside the project's boundaries.

50. Answer: C.

PMBOK® Guide, page 125, Section 5.5; and page 127, Section 5.5.2.1

Control Scope

Control Scope is the process of monitoring the status of the project and product scope and managing changes to the scope baseline. Controlling the project scope ensures all requested changes and recommended corrective or preventive actions are processed through the Perform Integrated Change Control process (see Section 4.5). Project scope control is also used to manage the actual changes when they occur and is integrated with the other control processes. Uncontrolled changes are often referred to as project scope creep. Change is inevitable, thereby mandating some type of change control process.

Variance Analysis

Project performance measurements are used to assess the magnitude of variation from the original scope baseline. Important aspects of project scope control include determining the cause and degree of variance relative to the scope baseline (Section 5.3.3.3) and deciding whether corrective or preventive action is required.

51. Answer: A.
PMBOK® Guide, page 116, Section 5.3

Create WBS
Create WBS is the process of subdividing project deliverables and project work into smaller, more manageable components. The work breakdown structure (WBS) is a deliverable-oriented hierarchical decomposition of the work to be executed by the project team to accomplish the project objectives and create the required deliverables, with each descending level of the WBS representing an increasingly detailed definition of the project work. The WBS organizes and defines the total scope of the project, and represents the work specified in the current approved project scope statement.

52. Answer: A.
PMBOK® Guide, page 115, Section 5.2.3.1

Project Scope Statement
Project constraints. Lists and describes the specific project constraints associated with the project scope that limits the team's options, for example, a predefined budget or any imposed dates or schedule milestones that are issued by the customer or performing organization. When a project is performed under contract, contractual provisions will generally be constraints. Information on constraints may be listed in the project scope statement or in a separate log.

53. Answer: B.
PMBOK® Guide, page 112, Figure 5-4; and page 112, Section 5.2.1

Define Scope: Inputs
.1 Project Charter
.2 Requirements Documentation
.3 Organizational Process Assets

54. Answer: A.
PMBOK® Guide, page 116, Section 5.3

Create WBS
Create WBS is the process of subdividing project deliverables and project work into smaller, more manageable components. The work breakdown structure (WBS) is a deliverable-oriented hierarchical decomposition of the work to be executed by the project team to accomplish the project objectives and create the required deliverables, with each descending level of the WBS representing an increasingly detailed definition of the project work. The WBS organizes and defines the total scope of the project, and represents the work specified in the current approved project scope statement.

55. Answer: B.
PMBOK® Guide, page 116, Section 5.3

Create WBS
Create WBS is the process of subdividing project deliverables and project work into smaller, more manageable components. The work breakdown structure (WBS) is a deliverable-oriented hierarchical decomposition of the work to be executed by the project team to accomplish the project objectives and create the required deliverables, with each descending level of the WBS representing an increasingly detailed definition of the project work. The WBS organizes and defines the total scope of the project, and represents the work specified in the current approved project scope statement.

56. Answer: C.
PMBOK® Guide page 112, Figure 5-4; and pages 115–116, Section 5.2.3

Define Scope: Outputs
.1 Project Scope Statement
.2 Project Document Updates

57. Answer: A.
PMBOK® Guide, page 123, Section 5.4

Verify Scope
Verify Scope is the process of formalizing acceptance of the completed project deliverables. Verifying scope includes reviewing deliverables with the customer or sponsor to ensure that they are completed satisfactorily and obtaining formal acceptance of deliverables by the customer or sponsor. Scope verification differs from quality control in that scope verification is primarily concerned with acceptance of the deliverables, while quality control is primarily concerned with correctness of the deliverables and meeting the quality requirements specified for the deliverables. Quality control is generally performed before scope verification, but these two processes can be performed in parallel.

58. Answer: D.
PMBOK® Guide, page 125, Figure 5-13; page 128, Section 5.5.3; page 123, Figure 5-11; and page 125, Section 5.4.3

Control Scope: Outputs
.1 Work Performance Measurements
.2 Organizational Process Assets Updates
.3 Change Requests
.4 Project Management Plan Updates
.5 Project Document Updates

Verify Scope: Outputs
.1 Accepted Deliverables
.2 Change Requests
.3 Project Document Updates

Project Time Management
(Chapter 6 of the *PMBOK® Guide*)

59. Answer: B.
PMBOK® Guide, page 129, Introduction; and page 131, Figure 6-1

Project Time Management
Project Time Management includes the processes required to manage timely completion of the project. Figure 6-1 provides an overview of the Project Time Management processes, which are as follows:

6.1 Define Activities—The process of identifying the specific actions to be performed to produce the project deliverables.

6.2 Sequence Activities—The process of identifying and documenting relationships among the project activities.

6.3 Estimate Activity Resources—The process of estimating the type and quantities of material, people, equipment, or supplies required to perform each activity.

6.4 Estimate Activity Durations—The process of approximating the number of work periods needed to complete individual activities with estimated resources.

6.5 Develop Schedule—The process of analyzing activity sequences, durations, resource requirements, and schedule constraints to create the project schedule.

6.6 Control Schedule—The process of monitoring the status of the project to update project progress and managing changes to the schedule baseline.

60. Answer: B.
PMBOK® Guide, page 135, Section 6.1.2.2

Rolling Wave Planning
Rolling wave planning is a form of progressive elaboration planning where the work to be accomplished in the near term is planned in detail and future work is planned at a higher level of the WBS. Therefore, work can exist at various levels of detail depending on where it is in the project life cycle. For example, during early strategic planning, when information is less defined, work packages may be decomposed to the milestone level. As more is known about the upcoming events in the near term it can be decomposed into activities.

61. Answer: A.
PMBOK® Guide, page 138, Section 6.2.2.1

Precedence Diagramming Method (PDM)
PDM is a method used in Critical Path Methodology (CPM) for constructing a project schedule network diagram that uses boxes or rectangles, referred to as nodes, to represent activities, and connects them with arrows that show the logical relationships that exist between them. Figure 6-7 shows a simple project schedule network diagram drawn using PDM. This technique is also called Activity-On-Node (AON), and is the method used by most project management software packages.

62. Answer: D.
PMBOK® Guide, page 148, Section 6.4.1.3

Activity Resource Requirements
The estimated activity resource requirements (Section 6.3.3.1) will have an effect on the duration of the activity, since the resources assigned to the activity and the availability of those resources will significantly influence the duration of most activities. For example, if additional or lower-skilled resources are assigned to an activity, there may be reduced efficiency or productivity due to increased communication, training, and coordination needs.

63. Answer: B.
PMBOK® Guide, page 157, Section 6.5.2.7

Schedule Compression
Fast tracking. A schedule compression technique in which phases or activities normally performed in sequence are performed in parallel. An example is constructing the foundation for a building before completing all of the architectural drawings. Fast tracking may result in rework and increased risk. Fast tracking only works if activities can be overlapped to shorten the duration.

64. Answer: B.
PMBOK® Guide, pages 139–140, Section 6.2.2.2

> **Mandatory dependencies.** Mandatory dependencies
> are those that are contractually required or inherent in
> the nature of the work. The project team determines
> which dependencies are mandatory during the process
> of sequencing the activities. Mandatory dependencies
> often involve physical limitations, such as on a
> construction project where it is impossible to erect the
> superstructure until after the foundation has been built,
> or on an electronics project, where a prototype must
> be built before it can be tested. Mandatory
> dependencies are also sometimes referred to as hard
> logic.

> **Discretionary dependencies.** The project team
> determines which dependencies are discretionary
> during the process of sequencing the activities.
> Discretionary dependencies are sometimes referred to
> as preferred logic, preferential logic, or soft logic.
> Discretionary dependencies are established based on
> knowledge of best practices within a particular
> application area or some unusual aspect of the project
> where a specific sequence is desired, even though
> there may be other acceptable sequences.

65. Answer: D.
PMBOK® Guide, pages 133–136, Figure 6-3 and Section
6.1.1

> **Define Activities: Inputs**
> **.1 Scope Baseline**
> **.2 Enterprise Environmental Factors**
> **.3 Organizational Process Assets**

66. Answer: A.
PMBOK® Guide, page 156, Section 6.5.2.7

Schedule Compression
Crashing. A schedule compression technique in which cost and schedule tradeoffs are analyzed to determine how to obtain the greatest amount of compression for the least incremental cost. Examples of crashing could include approving overtime, bringing in additional resources, or paying to expedite delivery to activities on the critical path. Crashing only works for activities where additional resources will shorten the duration. Crashing does not always produce a viable alternative and may result in increased risk and/or cost.

67. Answer: B.
PMBOK® Guide, page 157, Section 6.5.3.1

Project Schedule
Bar charts. These charts, with bars representing activities, show activity start and end dates, as well as expected durations. Bar charts are relatively easy to read, and are frequently used in management presentations. For control and management communication, the broader, more comprehensive summary activity, sometimes referred to as a hammock activity, is used between milestones or across multiple interdependent work packages, and is displayed in bar chart reports.

68. Answer: C.
PMBOK® Guide, page 138, Section 6.2.2.1

Precedence Diagramming Method (PDM)
PDM is a method used in Critical Path Methodology (CPM) for constructing a project schedule network diagram that uses boxes or rectangles, referred to as nodes, to represent activities, and connects them with arrows that show the logical relationships that exist between them.

69. Answer: B.
PMBOK® Guide, pages 154–155, Section 6.5.2.2

Critical Path Method
The critical path method calculates the theoretical early start and finish dates, and late start and finish dates, for all activities without regard for any resource limitations, by performing a forward and backward pass analysis through the schedule network. The resulting early and late start and finish dates are not necessarily the project schedule; rather, they indicate the time periods within which the activity could be scheduled, given activity durations, logical relationships, leads, lags, and other known constraints.

Calculated early start and finish dates, and late start and finish dates, may be affected by activity total float, which provides schedule flexibility and, may be positive, negative, or zero. On any network path, the schedule flexibility is measured by the positive difference between early and late dates, and is termed "total float." Critical paths have either a zero or negative total float, and schedule activities on a critical path are called "critical activities." A critical path is normally characterized by zero total float on the critical path. Networks can have multiple near critical paths.

70. Answer: D.
PMBOK® Guide, page 156, Section 6.5.2.4; and page 163, Section 6.6.2.4

Resource Leveling
Resource leveling is a schedule network analysis technique applied to a schedule that has already been analyzed by the critical path method. Resource leveling can be used when shared or critical required resources are only available at certain times, are only available in limited quantities, or to keep resource usage at a constant level. Resource leveling is necessary when resources have been over-allocated, such as when a resource has been assigned to two or more activities during the same time period, when shared or critical required resources are only available at certain times or are only available in limited quantities. Resource leveling can often cause the original critical path to change.

Resource Leveling
Resource leveling as described in Section 6.5.2.4, is used to optimize the distribution of work among resources.

71. Answer: B.
PMBOK® Guide, page 155, Section 6.5.2.3

Critical Chain Method
Critical chain is a schedule network analysis technique that modifies the project schedule to account for limited resources. Initially, the project schedule network diagram is built using duration estimates with required dependencies and defined constraints as inputs. The critical path is then calculated. After the critical path is identified, resource availability is entered and the resource-limited schedule result is determined. The resulting schedule often has an altered critical path.

72. Answer: A.
PMBOK® Guide, page 156, Section 6.5.2.7; and Glossary

Schedule Compression
Crashing. A schedule compression technique in which cost and schedule tradeoffs are analyzed to determine how to obtain the greatest amount of compression for the least incremental cost. Examples of crashing could include approving overtime, bringing in additional resources, or paying to expedite delivery to activities on the critical path. Crashing only works for activities where additional resources will shorten the duration. Crashing does not always produce a viable alternative and may result in increased risk and/or cost.
Crashing [Technique]. A specific type of project schedule compression technique performed by taking action to decrease the total project schedule duration after analyzing a number of alternatives to determine how to get the maximum schedule duration compression for the least additional cost. Typical approaches for crashing a schedule include reducing schedule activity durations and increasing the assignment of resources on schedule activities. See also *fast tracking* and *schedule compression*.

73. Answer: C.
PMBOK® Guide, page 142, Figure 6-8 and pages 143–144, Section 6.3.1

Estimate Activity Resources: Inputs
.1 Activity List
.2 Activity Attributes
.3 Resource Calendars
.4 Enterprise Environmental Factors
.5 Organizational Process Assets

74. Answer: C.

PMBOK® Guide, page 145, Section 6.3.3.1; and page 219, Section 9.1.1.1

Activity Resource Requirements

The output of the Estimate Activity Resources process identifies the types and quantities of resources required for each activity in a work package. These requirements can then be aggregated to determine the estimated resources for each work package. The amount of detail and the level of specificity of the resource requirement descriptions can vary by application area.

Activity Resource Requirements

Human resource planning uses activity resource requirements (Section 6.3.3.1) to determine the human resource needs for the project. The preliminary requirements regarding the required people and competencies for the project team members are progressively elaborated as part of the human resource planning process.

75. Answer: D.
PMBOK® Guide, page 140, Section 6.2.2.3

Applying Leads and Lags
The project management team determines the dependencies that may require a lead or a lag to accurately define the logical relationship. The use of leads and lags should not replace schedule logic. Activities and their related assumptions should be documented.

A lead allows an acceleration of the successor activity. For example, on a project to construct a new office building, the landscaping could be scheduled to start 2 weeks prior to the scheduled punch list completion. This would be shown as a finish-to-start with a 2-week lead.

A lag directs a delay in the successor activity. For example, a technical writing team can begin editing the draft of a large document 15 days after they begin writing it. This could be shown as a start-to-start relationship with a 15-day lag.

76. Answer: B.
PMBOK® Guide, pages 150–151, Section 6.4.2.4; and Glossary

Three-Point Estimates
The accuracy of activity duration estimates can be improved by considering estimation uncertainty and risk. This concept originated with the Program Evaluation and Review Technique (PERT). PERT uses three estimates to define an approximate range for an activity's duration:
- Most likely.
- Optimistic.
- Pessimistic.

PERT analysis calculates an **Expected** (t_E) activity duration using a weighted average of these three estimates.

Program Evaluation and Review Technique (PERT). A technique for estimating that applies a weighted average of optimistic, pessimistic, and most likely estimates when there is uncertainty with the individual activity estimates.

77. Answer: B.

PMBOK® Guide, page 149, Section 6.4.2.2

Analogous Estimating

Analogous estimating uses parameters such as duration, budget, size, weight, and complexity, from a previous, similar project, as the basis for estimating the same parameter or measure for a future project. When estimating durations, this technique relies on the actual duration of previous, similar projects as the basis for estimating the duration of the current project. It is a gross value estimating approach, sometimes adjusted for known differences in project complexity.

Analogous duration estimating is frequently used to estimate project duration when there is a limited amount of detailed information about the project for example, in the early phases of a project. Analogous estimating uses historical information and expert judgment.

Analogous estimating is generally less costly and time consuming than other techniques, but it is also generally less accurate.

78. Answer: D.
PMBOK® Guide, page 155, Section 6.5.2.3

Critical Chain Method
The critical chain method adds duration buffers that are non-work schedule activities to manage uncertainty. One buffer, placed at the end of the critical chain, is known as the project buffer and protects the target finish date from slippage along the critical chain. Additional buffers, known as feeding buffers, are placed at each point that a chain of dependent tasks not on the critical chain feeds into the critical chain. Feeding buffers thus protect the critical chain from slippage along the feeding chains. The size of each buffer should account for the uncertainty in the duration of the chain of dependent tasks leading up to that buffer. Once the buffer schedule activities are determined, the planned activities are scheduled to their latest possible planned start and finish dates. Consequently, in lieu of managing the total float of network paths, the critical chain method focuses on managing remaining buffer durations against the remaining durations of task chains.

Project Cost Management

79. Answer: B.

PMBOK® Guide, page 165, Introduction

Project Cost Management

Project Cost Management includes the processes involved in estimating, budgeting, and controlling costs so that the project can be completed within the approved budget. Figure 7-1 provides an overview of the Project Cost Management processes which include the following:

7.1 Estimate Costs—The process of developing an approximation of the monetary resources needed to complete project activities.

7.2 Determine Budget—The process of aggregating the estimated costs of individual activities or work packages to establish an authorized cost baseline.

7.3 Control Costs—The process of monitoring the status of the project to update the project budget and managing changes to the cost baseline.

80. Answer: C.
PMBOK® Guide, page 168, Section 7.1; and page 170, Section 7.1.1.4

Estimate Costs
Estimate Costs is the process of developing an approximation of the monetary resources needed to complete project activities.

Cost estimates are generally expressed in units of some currency (i.e., dollars, euro, yen, etc.), although in some instances other units of measure, such as staff hours or staff days, are used to facilitate comparisons by eliminating the effects of currency fluctuations.

Sources of input information are derived from the outputs of project processes in other Knowledge Areas. Once received, all of this information will remain available as inputs to all three of the cost management processes.

Costs are estimated for all resources that will be charged to the project. This includes, but is not limited to, labor, materials, equipment, services, and facilities, as well as special categories such as an inflation allowance or contingency costs. A cost estimate is a quantitative assessment of the likely costs for resources required to complete the activity.

Risk Register
The risk register (Section 11.2.3.1) should be reviewed to consider risk mitigation costs. Risks, which can be either threats or opportunities, typically have an impact on both activity and overall project costs. As a general rule, when the project experiences a negative risk event, the near-term cost of the project will usually increase, and there will sometimes be a delay in the project schedule.

81. Answer: D

PMBOK® Guide, page 179–180, Section 7.3

Control Costs

Project cost control includes:

- Influencing the factors that create changes to the authorized cost baseline,
- Ensuring that all change requests are acted on in a timely manner,
- Managing the actual changes when and as they occur,
- Ensuring that cost expenditures do not exceed the authorized funding, by period and in total for the project,
- Monitoring cost performance to isolate and understand variances from the approved cost baseline,
- Monitoring work performance against funds expended,
- Preventing unapproved changes from being included in the reported cost or resource usage,
- Informing appropriate stakeholders of all approved changes and associated cost, and
- Acting to bring expected cost overruns within acceptable limits.

82. Answer: D.

PMBOK® Guide, page 168, Section 7.1

Estimate Costs

Costs are estimated for all resources that will be charged to the project. This includes, but is not limited to, labor, materials, equipment, services, and facilities, as well as special categories such as an inflation allowance or contingency costs. A cost estimate is a quantitative assessment of the likely costs for resources required to complete the activity.

83. Answer: C.
PMBOK® Guide, page 172, Section 7.1.2.3

Parametric Estimating
Parametric estimating uses a statistical relationship between historical data and other variables (e.g., square footage in construction) to calculate an estimate for activity parameters, such as cost, budget, and duration. This technique can produce higher levels of accuracy depending upon the sophistication and underlying data built into the model. Parametric cost estimates can be applied to a total project or to segments of a project, in conjunction with other estimating methods.

84. Answer: B.
PMBOK® Guide, page 171–172, Section 7.1.2.2

Analogous Estimating
Analogous cost estimating uses the values of parameters, such as scope, cost, budget, and duration or measures of scale such as size, weight, and complexity, from a previous, similar project as the basis for estimating the same parameter or measure for a current project. When estimating costs, this technique relies on the actual cost of previous, similar projects as the basis for estimating the cost of the current project. It is a gross value estimating approach, sometimes adjusted for known differences in project complexity.

Analogous cost estimating is frequently used to estimate a parameter when there is a limited amount of detailed information about the project, for example, in the early phases of a project. Analogous cost estimating uses historical information and expert judgment.

85. Answer: C.
PMBOK® Guide, page 174, Section 7.2; and pages 179–180, Section 7.3

Determine Budget
Determine Budget is the process of aggregating the estimated costs of individual activities or work packages to establish an authorized cost baseline. This baseline includes all authorized budgets, but excludes management reserves.

Control Costs
Control Costs is the process of monitoring the status of the project to update the project budget and managing changes to the cost baseline... The key to effective cost control is the management of the approved cost performance baseline and the changes to that baseline.

Project cost control includes:
• Influencing the factors that create changes to the authorized cost baseline...

86. Answer: D.
PMBOK® Guide, page 184, Section 7.3.2.2

EAC forecast for ETC work performed at the budgeted rate. This EAC method accepts the actual project performance to date (whether favorable or unfavorable) as represented by the actual costs, and predicts that all future ETC work will be accomplished at the budgeted rate. When actual performance is unfavorable, the assumption that future performance will improve should be accepted only when supported by project risk analysis. Equation: $EAC = AC + BAC - EV$.

87. Answer: C.
PMBOK® Guide, page 184, Section 7.3.2.2

EAC forecast for ETC work performed at the present CPI. This method assumes what the project has experienced to date can be expected to continue in the future. The ETC work is assumed to be performed at the same cumulative cost performance index (CPI) as that incurred by the project to date. Equation: $EAC = BAC / \text{cumulative CPI}$.

88. Answer: B.
PMBOK® Guide, page 178, Section 7.2.3.1, and Figure 7-6

Cost Performance Baseline
The cost performance baseline is an authorized time-phased budget at completion (BAC) used to measure, monitor, and control overall cost performance on the project. It is developed as a summation of the approved budgets by time period and is typically displayed in the form of an S-curve, as is illustrated in Figure 7-6. In the earned value management technique the cost performance baseline is referred to as the performance measurement baseline (PMB).

89. Answer: D.
PMBOK® Guide, page 184, Section 7.3.2.2

Forecasting
As the project progresses, the project team can develop a forecast for the estimate at completion (EAC) that may differ from the budget at completion (BAC) based on the project performance. If it becomes obvious that the BAC is no longer viable, the project manager should develop a forecasted EAC. Forecasting the EAC involves making estimates or predictions of conditions and events in the project's future based on information and knowledge available at the time of the forecast. Forecasts are generated, updated, and reissued based on work performance information (Section 4.3.3.2) provided as the project is executed. The work performance information covers the project's past performance and any information that could impact the project in the future.

EACs are typically based on the actual costs incurred for work completed, plus an estimate to complete (ETC) the remaining work. It is incumbent on the project team to predict what it may encounter to perform the ETC, based on its experience to date.

90. Answer: A.
PMBOK® Guide, pages 165–166, Introduction

Project Cost Management
The work involved in performing the three processes of Project Cost Management is preceded by a planning effort of the project management team. This planning effort is part of the Develop Project Management Plan process (Section 4.2), which produces a cost management plan that sets out the format and establishes the criteria for planning, structuring, estimating, budgeting, and controlling project costs. The cost management processes and their associated tools and techniques are usually selected during the project life cycle definition (Section 2.1), and are documented in the cost management plan. For example, the cost management plan can establish the following:

- Level of accuracy. . .
- Units of measure. . .
- Organizational procedures links. . .
- Control thresholds. Variance thresholds for monitoring cost performance may be specified to indicate an agreed-upon amount of variation to be allowed before some action needs to be taken. Thresholds are typically expressed as percentage deviations from the baseline plan.
- Rules of performance measurement. . .
- Reporting formats. . .
- Process descriptions. . .
- All of this information is included in the cost management plan, a component of the project management plan, either as text within the body of the plan or as appendices. The cost management plan may be formal or informal, highly detailed or broadly framed, based upon the needs of the project.

91. Answer: C.

PMBOK® Guide, pages 181–183, Section 7.3.2.1 and Figure 7-9; and page 271, Figure 10-15

Earned Value Management

Variances from the approved baseline will also be monitored:

- **Schedule variance.** Schedule variance (SV) is a measure of schedule performance on a project. It is equal to the earned value (EV) minus the planned value (PV). The EVM schedule variance is a useful metric in that it can indicate a project falling behind its baseline schedule. The EVM schedule variance will ultimately equal zero when the project is completed because all of the planned values will have been earned. EVM SVs are best used in conjunction with critical path methodology (CPM) scheduling and risk management. Equation: $SV = EV - PV$.

- **Cost variance**
  The SV and CV values can be converted to efficiency indicators to reflect the cost and schedule performance of any project for comparison against all other projects or within a portfolio of projects. The variances and indices are useful for determining project status and providing a basis for estimating project cost and schedule outcome.

- **Schedule performance index.** The schedule performance index (SPI) is a measure of progress achieved compared to progress planned on a project. It is sometimes used in conjunction with the cost performance index (CPI) to forecast the final project completion estimates. An SPI value less than 1.0 indicates less work was completed than was planned. An SPI greater than 1.0 indicates that more work was completed than was planned. Since the SPI measures all project work, the performance on the critical path must also be analyzed to determine whether the project will finish ahead of or behind its planned finish date. The SPI is equal to the ratio of the EV to the PV. Equation: $SPI = EV/PV$.

- **Cost performance index**. . .
  The three parameters of planned value, earned value, and actual cost can be monitored and reported on both a period-by-period basis (typically weekly or monthly) and on a cumulative basis. Figure 7-9 uses S-curves to display EV data for a project that is performing over budget and behind the work plan.

92. Answer: A.

PMBOK® Guide, pages 181–183, Section 7.3.2.1 and Figure 7-9; and page 271, Figure 10-15

Earned Value Management

Variances from the approved baseline will also be monitored:
- Schedule variance. . .
- Cost variance. Cost variance (CV) is a measure of cost performance on a project. It is equal to the earned value (EV) minus the actual costs (AC). The cost variance at the end of the project will be the difference between the budget at completion (BAC) and the actual amount spent. The EVM CV is particularly critical because it indicates the relationship of physical performance to the costs spent. Any negative EVM CV is often non-recoverable to the project. Equation: $CV = EV - AC$.

The SV and CV values can be converted to efficiency indicators to reflect the cost and schedule performance of any project for comparison against all other projects or within a portfolio of projects. The variances and indices are useful for determining project status and providing a basis for estimating project cost and schedule outcome.
- Schedule performance index. . .
- Cost performance index. The cost performance index (CPI) is a measure of the value of work completed compared to the actual cost or progress made on the project. It is considered the most critical EVM metric and measures the cost efficiency for the work completed. A CPI value less than 1.0 indicates a cost overrun for work completed. A CPI value greater than 1.0 indicates a cost underrun of performance to date. The CPI is equal to the ratio of the EV to the AC. Equation: $CPI = EV/AC$.

The three parameters of planned value, earned value, and actual cost can be monitored and reported on both a period-by-period basis (typically weekly or monthly) and on a cumulative basis. Figure 7-9 uses S-curves to display EV data for a project that is performing over budget and behind the work plan.

93. Answer: C.
PMBOK® Guide, page 181, Section 7.3.2.1

Earned Value Management

Earned value management (EVM) in its various forms is a commonly used method of performance measurement. It integrates project scope, cost, and schedule measures to help the project management team assess and measure project performance and progress. It is a project management technique that requires the formation of an integrated baseline against which performance can be measured for the duration of the project. The principles of EVM can be applied to all projects, in any industry.

94. Answer: D.

PMBOK® Guide, pages 181–183, Section 7.3.2.1 and Figure 7-9

Earned Value Management

Variances from the approved baseline will also be monitored:

- **Schedule variance.** Schedule variance (SV) is a measure of schedule performance on a project. It is equal to the earned value (EV) minus the planned value (PV). The EVM schedule variance is a useful metric in that it can indicate a project falling behind its baseline schedule. The EVM schedule variance will ultimately equal zero when the project is completed because all of the planned values will have been earned. EVM SVs are best used in conjunction with critical path methodology (CPM) scheduling and risk management. Equation: SV = EV − PV.
- **Cost variance.** Cost variance (CV) is a measure of cost performance on a project. It is equal to the earned value (EV) minus the actual costs (AC). The cost variance at the end of the project will be the difference between the budget at completion (BAC) and the actual amount spent. The EVM CV is particularly critical because it indicates the relationship of physical performance to the costs spent. Any negative EVM CV is often non-recoverable to the project. Equation: CV = EV − AC.

The SV and CV values can be converted to efficiency indicators to reflect the cost and schedule performance of any project for comparison against all other projects or within a portfolio of projects. The variances and indices are useful for determining project status and providing a basis for estimating project cost and schedule outcome.

- **Schedule performance index.** The schedule performance index (SPI) is a measure of progress achieved compared to progress planned on a project. It is sometimes used in conjunction with the cost performance index (CPI) to forecast the final project completion estimates. An SPI value less than 1.0 indicates less work was completed than was planned. An SPI greater than 1.0 indicates that more work was completed than was planned. Since the SPI measures all project work, the performance on the critical path must also be analyzed to determine whether the project will finish ahead of or behind its planned finish date. The SPI is equal to the ratio of the EV to the PV. Equation: SPI = EV/PV.
- **Cost performance index.** The cost performance index (CPI) is a measure of the value of work completed compared to the actual cost or progress made on the project. It is considered the most critical EVM metric and measures the cost efficiency for the work completed. A CPI value less than 1.0 indicates a cost overrun for work completed. A CPI value greater than 1.0 indicates a cost underrun of performance to date. The CPI is equal to the ratio of the EV to the AC. Equation: CPI = EV/AC.

The three parameters of planned value, earned value, and actual cost can be monitored and reported on both a period-by-period basis (typically weekly or monthly) and on a cumulative basis. Figure 7-9 uses S-curves to display EV data for a project that is performing over budget and behind the work plan.

95. Answer: B.

PMBOK® Guide, pages 181–183, Section 7.3.2.1 and Figure 7-9

Earned Value Management

Cost variance. Cost variance (CV) is a measure of cost performance on a project. It is equal to the earned value (EV) minus the actual costs (AC). The cost variance at the end of the project will be the difference between the budget at completion (BAC) and the actual amount spent. The EVM CV is particularly critical because it indicates the relationship of physical performance to the costs spent. Any negative EVM CV is often non-recoverable to the project. Equation: $CV = EV - AC$.

96. Answer: B.
PMBOK® Guide, pages 181–183, Section 7.3.2.1; and Glossary

Earned Value Management
. . .EVM develops and monitors three key dimensions for each work package and control account:
. . .

Earned value. Earned value (EV) is the value of work performed expressed in terms of the approved budget assigned to that work for an activity or work breakdown structure component. It is the authorized work that has been completed, plus the authorized budget for such completed work. The EV being measured must be related to the PV baseline (PMB), and the EV measured cannot be greater than the authorized PV budget for a component. The term EV is often used to describe the percentage completion of a project. A progress measurement criteria should be established for each WBS component to measure work in progress. Project managers monitor EV, both incrementally to determine current status and cumulatively to determine the long-term performance trends.

Earned Value (EV). The value of work performed expressed in terms of the approved budget assigned to that work for a schedule activity or work breakdown structure component. Also referred to as the budgeted cost of work performed (BCWP).

97. Answer: B.

PMBOK® Guide, pages 181–183, Section 7.3.2.1 and Figure 7-9

Earned Value Management

The SV and CV values can be converted to efficiency indicators to reflect the cost and schedule performance of any project for comparison against all other projects or within a portfolio of projects. The variances and indices are useful for determining project status and providing a basis for estimating project cost and schedule outcome.

- **Schedule performance index.** The schedule performance index (SPI) is a measure of progress achieved compared to progress planned on a project. It is sometimes used in conjunction with the cost performance index (CPI) to forecast the final project completion estimates. An SPI value less than 1.0 indicates less work was completed than was planned. An SPI greater than 1.0 indicates that more work was completed than was planned. Since the SPI measures all project work, the performance on the critical path must also be analyzed to determine whether the project will finish ahead of or behind its planned finish date. The SPI is equal to the ratio of the EV to the PV. Equation: SPI = EV/PV.

- **Cost performance index.** The cost performance index (CPI) is a measure of the value of work completed compared to the actual cost or progress made on the project. It is considered the most critical EVM metric and measures the cost efficiency for the work completed. A CPI value less than 1.0 indicates a cost overrun for work completed. A CPI value greater than 1.0 indicates a cost underrun of performance to date. The CPI is equal to the ratio of the EV to the AC. Equation: CPI = EV/AC.

The three parameters of planned value, earned value, and actual cost can be monitored and reported on both a period-by-period basis (typically weekly or monthly) and on a cumulative basis. Figure 7-9 uses S-curves to display EV data for a project that is performing over budget and behind the work plan.

98. Answer: D.

PMBOK® Guide, pages 181–183, Section 7.3.2.1 and Figure 7-9

Earned Value Management

The SV and CV values can be converted to efficiency indicators to reflect the cost and schedule performance of any project for comparison against all other projects or within a portfolio of projects. The variances and indices are useful for determining project status and providing a basis for estimating project cost and schedule outcome.

- **Schedule performance index.** The schedule performance index (SPI) is a measure of progress achieved compared to progress planned on a project. It is sometimes used in conjunction with the cost performance index (CPI) to forecast the final project completion estimates. An SPI value less than 1.0 indicates less work was completed than was planned. An SPI greater than 1.0 indicates that more work was completed than was planned. Since the SPI measures all project work, the performance on the critical path must also be analyzed to determine whether the project will finish ahead of or behind its planned finish date. The SPI is equal to the ratio of the EV to the PV. Equation: SPI = EV/PV.

- **Cost performance index.** The cost performance index (CPI) is a measure of the value of work completed compared to the actual cost or progress made on the project. It is considered the most critical EVM metric and measures the cost efficiency for the work completed. A CPI value less than 1.0 indicates a cost overrun for work completed. A CPI value greater than 1.0 indicates a cost underrun of performance to date. The CPI is equal to the ratio of the EV to the AC. Equation: CPI = EV/AC.

The three parameters of planned value, earned value, and actual cost can be monitored and reported on both a period-by-period basis (typically weekly or monthly) and on a cumulative basis. Figure 7-9 uses S-curves to display EV data for a project that is performing over budget and behind the work plan.

99. Answer: D.
PMBOK® Guide, pages 181–183, Section 7.3.2.1 and Figure 7-9

Earned Value Management
The SV and CV values can be converted to efficiency indicators to reflect the cost and schedule performance of any project for comparison against all other projects or within a portfolio of projects. The variances and indices are useful for determining project status and providing a basis for estimating project cost and schedule outcome.

- **Schedule performance index.** The schedule performance index (SPI) is a measure of progress achieved compared to progress planned on a project. It is sometimes used in conjunction with the cost performance index (CPI) to forecast the final project completion estimates. An SPI value less than 1.0 indicates less work was completed than was planned. An SPI greater than 1.0 indicates that more work was completed than was planned. Since the SPI measures all project work, the performance on the critical path must also be analyzed to determine whether the project will finish ahead of or behind its planned finish date. The SPI is equal to the ratio of the EV to the PV. Equation: $SPI = EV/PV$.

- **Cost performance index.** The cost performance index (CPI) is a measure of the value of work completed compared to the actual cost or progress made on the project. It is considered the most critical EVM metric and measures the cost efficiency for the work completed. A CPI value less than 1.0 indicates a cost overrun for work completed. A CPI value greater than 1.0 indicates a cost underrun of performance to date. The CPI is equal to the ratio of the EV to the AC. Equation: $CPI = EV/AC$.

The three parameters of planned value, earned value, and actual cost can be monitored and reported on both a period-by-period basis (typically weekly or monthly) and on a cumulative basis. Figure 7-9 uses S-curves to display EV data for a project that is performing over budget and behind the work plan.

Project Quality Management
(Chapter 8 of the *PMBOK® Guide*)

100. Answer: A.
PMBOK® Guide, page 190, Introduction

Project Quality Management
Modern quality management complements project management. Both disciplines recognize the importance of:
- **Customer satisfaction.** Understanding, evaluating, defining, and managing expectations so that customer requirements are met. This requires a combination of conformance to requirements (to ensure the project produces what it was created to produce) and fitness for use (the product or service must satisfy real needs).

101. Answer: C.
PMBOK® Guide, page 190, Introduction

Project Quality Management
Prevention over inspection. One of the fundamental tenets of modern quality management states that quality is planned, designed, and built in—not inspected in. The cost of preventing mistakes is generally much less than the cost of correcting them when they are found by inspection.

102. Answer: D.
PMBOK® Guide, page 195, Section 8.1.2.1

Cost-Benefit Analysis
The primary benefits of meeting quality requirements can include less rework, higher productivity, lower costs, and increased stakeholder satisfaction. A business case for each quality activity compares the cost of the quality step to the expected benefit.

103. Answer: D.
PMBOK® Guide, pages 206–208, Section 8.3.1 and Figure 8-10

Perform Quality Control: Inputs
.1 Project Management Plan
.2 Quality Metrics
.3 Quality Checklists
.4 Work Performance Measurements
.5 Approved Change Requests
.6 Deliverables
.7 Organizational Process Assets

104. Answer: B.
PMBOK® Guide, page 197, Section 8.1.2.5

Design of Experiments
Design of experiments (DOE) is a statistical method for identifying which factors may influence specific variables of a product or process under development or in production. DOE should be used during the Plan Quality process to determine the number and type of tests and their impact on cost of quality.

105. Answer: A.
PMBOK® Guide, page 200, Section 8.1.3.1

Quality Management Plan
The quality management plan describes how the project management team will implement the performing organization's quality policy. It is a component or a subsidiary plan of the project management plan.

The quality management plan provides input to the overall project management plan and includes quality control, quality assurance, and continuous process improvement approaches for the project.

106. Answer: C.
PMBOK® Guide, page 201, Section 8.2

Perform Quality Assurance
Perform Quality Assurance is the process of auditing the quality requirements and the results from quality control measurements to ensure appropriate quality standards and operational definitions are used.

107. Answer: D.
PMBOK® Guide, pages 210–211, Section 8.3.2.5 and Figure 8-15

Pareto Chart
A Pareto chart, also referred to as a Pareto diagram, is a specific type of histogram, ordered by frequency of occurrence. It shows how many defects were generated by type or category of identified cause (Figure 8-15). Rank ordering is used to focus corrective action. The project team should address the causes creating the greatest number of defects first.

108. Answer: D.
PMBOK® Guide, page 195, Section 8.1.2.2 and Figure 8-4

Cost of Quality (COQ)
Cost of quality includes all costs incurred over the life of the product by investment in preventing nonconformance to requirements, appraising the product or service for conformance to requirements, and failing to meet requirements (rework). Failure costs are often categorized into internal (found by the project) and external (found by the customer). Failure costs are also called cost of poor quality. Figure 8-4 provides some examples to consider in each area.

109. Answer: A.
PMBOK® Guide, page 191, Introduction

Project Quality Management
Cost of quality (COQ) refers to the total cost of all efforts related to quality throughout the product life cycle. Project decisions can impact operational costs of quality as a result of product returns, warranty claims, and recall campaigns. Therefore, due to the temporary nature of a project, the sponsoring organization may choose to invest in product quality improvement, especially defect prevention and appraisal, to reduce the external cost of quality.

110. Answer: D.
PMBOK® Guide, pages 206–213, Figure 8-5 and Section 8.3.2

Perform Quality Control: Tools and Techniques
The first seven of these tools and techniques are known as Ishikawa's seven basic tools of quality.
.1 Cause and Effect Diagrams
.2 Control Charts
.3 Flowcharting
.4 Histogram
.5 Pareto Chart
.6 Run Chart
.7 Scatter Diagram
.8 Statistical Sampling
.9 Inspection
.10 Approved Change Requests Review

111. Answer: A.
PMBOK® Guide, page 189, Introduction

Project Quality Management
Project Quality Management includes the processes and activities of the performing organization that determine quality policies, objectives, and responsibilities so that the project will satisfy the needs for which it was undertaken. It implements the quality management system through policy and procedures with continuous process improvement activities conducted throughout, as appropriate.

112. Answer: A.
PMBOK® Guide, page 190, Introduction

Project Quality Management
Quality and grade are not the same. Quality is "the degree to which a set of inherent characteristics fulfill requirements" Grade is a category assigned to products or services having the same functional use but different technical characteristics. While a quality level that fails to meet quality requirements is always a problem, low grade may not be. For example, a software product can be of high quality (no obvious defects, readable manual) and low grade (a limited number of features), or of low quality (many defects, poorly organized user documentation) and high grade (numerous features). The project manager and the project management team are responsible for managing the tradeoffs involved to deliver the required levels of both quality and grade.

113. Answer: C.
PMBOK® Guide, pages 196–197, Section 8.1.2.2 and
Figures 8-5 and 8-8; and page 209, Section 8.3.2.2

Control Charts
Control charts are used to determine whether or not a
process is stable or has predictable performance.

Control charts can be used to monitor various types of
output variables.

Control Charts
Control charts illustrate how a process behaves over
time and when a process is subject to special cause
variation, resulting in an out-of-control condition.

114. Answer: B.
PMBOK® Guide, page 201, Section 8.2

Perform Quality Assurance
Perform Quality Assurance is the process of auditing
the quality requirements and the results from quality
control measurements to ensure appropriate quality
standards and operational definitions are used.

115. Answer: B.
PMBOK® Guide, page 195, Section 8.1.2.1

Cost-Benefit Analysis
The primary benefits of meeting quality requirements
can include less rework, higher productivity, lower
costs, and increased stakeholder satisfaction. A
business case for each quality activity compares the
cost of the quality step to the expected benefit.

116. Answer: D.

PMBOK® Guide, page 197, Section 8.1.2.4

Benchmarking

Benchmarking involves comparing actual or planned project practices to those of comparable projects to identify best practices, generate ideas for improvement, and provide a basis for measuring performance. These other projects can be within the performing organization or outside of it and can be within the same or in another application area.

117. Answer: D.

PMBOK® Guide, page 191, Introduction

Project Quality Management

Continuous improvement. The plan-do-check-act cycle is the basis for quality improvement as defined by Shewhart and modified by Deming. In addition, quality improvement initiatives undertaken by the performing organization, such as TQM and Six Sigma, should improve the quality of the project's management as well as the quality of the project's product. Process improvement models include Malcolm Baldrige, Organizational Project Management Maturity Model (OPM3®), and Capability Maturity Model Integrated (CMMI®).

Project Human Resource Management
(Chapter 9 of the *PMBOK® Guide*)

118. Answer: D.
PMBOK® Guide, page 215, Introduction; and page 217, Figure 9-1

Project Human Resource Management
Figure 9-1 provides an overview of the Project Human Resource Management processes, which are as follows:

9.1 Develop Human Resource Plan—The process of identifying and documenting project roles, responsibilities, and required skills, reporting relationships and creating a staffing management plan.

9.2 Acquire Project Team—The process of confirming human resource availability and obtaining the team necessary to complete project assignments.

9.3 Develop Project Team—The process of improving the competencies, team interaction, and the overall team environment to enhance project performance.

9.4 Manage Project Team—The process of tracking team member performance, providing feedback, resolving issues, and managing changes to optimize project performance.

119. Answer: B.
PMBOK® Guide, page 225, Section 9.2; and page 227, Section 9.2.1.2

Acquire Project Team
Acquire Project Team is the process of confirming human resource availability and obtaining the team necessary to complete project assignments. . .

Enterprise Environmental Factors
The enterprise environmental factors that can influence the Acquire Project Team process include, but are not limited to:
- Existing information for human resources including who is available, their competency levels, their prior experience, their interest in working on the project and their cost rate;
- Personnel administration policies such as those that affect outsourcing;
- Organizational structure as described in Section 2.4.2; and
- Location or multiple locations.

120. Answer: C.
PMBOK® Guide, page 224, Section 9.1.3.1

Staff release plan. Determining the method and timing of releasing team members benefits both the project and team members. When team members are released from a project, the costs associated with those resources are no longer charged to the project, thus reducing project costs. Morale is improved when smooth transitions to upcoming projects are already planned. A staff release plan also helps mitigate human resource risks that may occur during or at the end of a project.

121. Answer: D.

PMBOK® Guide, page 225, Section 9.1.3.1; and page 234, Section 9.3.2.6

> *Recognition and rewards.* Clear criteria for rewards and a planned system for their use helps promote and reinforce desired behaviors. To be effective, recognition and rewards should be based on activities and performance under a person's control. For example, a team member who is to be rewarded for meeting cost objectives should have an appropriate level of control over decisions that affect expenses. Creating a plan with established times for distribution of rewards ensures that recognition takes place and is not forgotten. . .

> **Recognition and rewards**
> . . .Cultural differences should be considered when determining recognition and rewards. For example, developing appropriate team rewards in a culture that encourages individualism can be difficult.

> . . . However, the team members should not be punished for poor planning and consistently unrealistic expectations imposed by senior management. Win-lose (zero sum) rewards that only a limited number of project team members can achieve, such as team member of the month, can hurt team cohesiveness. Rewarding behavior that everyone can achieve, such as turning in progress reports on time, tends to increase support among team members.

122. Answer: B.
PMBOK® Guide, page 234, Section 9.3.2.5

Develop Project Team: Tools and Techniques
Co-location
Co-location involves placing many or all of the most active project team members in the same physical location to enhance their ability to perform as a team. Co-location can be temporary, such as at strategically important times during the project, or for the entire project. Co-location strategies can include a team meeting room, places to post schedules, and other conveniences that enhance communication and a sense of community. While co-location is considered a good strategy, the use of virtual teams is sometimes unavoidable.

123. Answer: C.
PMBOK® Guide, page 226, Figure 9-7; and pages 227–228, Section 9.2.2

Acquire Project Team: Tools and Techniques
.1 Pre-assignment
.2 Negotiation
.3 Acquisition
.4 Virtual Teams

124. Answer: D.
PMBOK® Guide, page 218, Figure 9-2; and pages 222–223, Section 9.1.3

Develop Human Resource Plan: Outputs
.1 Human Resource Plan
. . .The human resource plan should include, but not be limited to, the following:
- **Roles and responsibilities**
- **Project organization charts**
- **Staffing management plan**

125. Answer: C.
PMBOK® Guide, page 239, Section 9.4.2.3

Conflict Management
Conflict is inevitable in a project environment. Sources of conflict include scarce resources, scheduling priorities, and personal work styles. Team ground rules, group norms, and solid project management practices like communication planning and role definition, reduce the amount of conflict.

Successful conflict management results in greater productivity and positive working relationships. When managed properly, differences of opinion can lead to increased creativity and better decision making. If the differences become a negative factor, project team members are initially responsible for their resolution. If conflict escalates, the project manager should help facilitate a satisfactory resolution. Conflict should be addressed early and usually in private, using a direct, collaborative approach. If disruptive conflict continues, formal procedures may be used, including disciplinary actions.

126. Answer: C.
PMBOK® Guide, page 221, Section 9.1.2.1 and Figure 9-5

Matrix-based charts. A responsibility assignment matrix (RAM) is used to illustrate the connections between work packages or activities and project team members. On larger projects, RAMs can be developed at various levels. For example, a high-level RAM can define what a project team group or unit is responsible for within each component of the WBS, while lower-level RAMs are used within the group to designate roles, responsibilities, and levels of authority for specific activities. The matrix format shows all activities associated with one person and all people associated with one activity. This also ensures that there is only one person accountable for any one task to avoid confusion.

127. Answer: A.

PMBOK® Guide, pages 223–224, Section 9.1.3.1 and Figure 9-6

Staffing management plan. The staffing management plan, a part of the human resources plan within the project management plan, describes when and how human resource requirements will be met. . .

○ *Resource calendars*. The staffing management plan describes necessary time frames for project team members, either individually or collectively, as well as when acquisition activities such as recruiting should start. One tool for charting human resources is a resource histogram. This bar chart illustrates the number of hours a person, department, or entire project team will be needed each week or month over the course of the project. The chart can include a horizontal line that represents the maximum number of hours available from a particular resource. Bars that extend beyond the maximum available hours identify the need for a resource leveling strategy, such as adding more resources or modifying the schedule. An example of a resource histogram is illustrated in Figure 9-6.

128. Answer: B.
PMBOK® Guide, pages 232–233, Section 9.3.2.3; and Appendix G, Section G.2

Team-Building Activities
Team-building activities can vary from a five-minute agenda item in a status review meeting to an off-site, professionally facilitated experience designed to improve interpersonal relationships. The objective of team-building activities is to help individual team members work together effectively. Team-building strategies are particularly valuable when team members operate from remote locations without the benefit of face-to-face contact. . .

As an ongoing process, team building is crucial to project success. While team building is essential during the front end of a project, it is a never-ending process. Changes in a project environment are inevitable, and to manage them effectively a continued or a renewed team-building effort should be applied. The project manager should continually monitor team functioning and performance to determine if any actions are needed to prevent or correct various team problems.

Team Building
While team building is essential during the front end of a project, it is an ongoing process. Changes in a project environment are inevitable. To manage these changes effectively, a continued or renewed teambuilding effort is required. Outcomes of team building include mutual trust, high quality of information exchange, better decision making, and effective project control.

129. Answer: C.
PMBOK® Guide, page 232, Section 9.3.2.2

Training
Training includes all activities designed to enhance the competencies of the project team members. Training can be formal or informal. Examples of training methods include classroom, online, computer-based, on-the-job training from another project team member, mentoring, and coaching. If project team members lack necessary management or technical skills, such skills can be developed as part of the project work. Scheduled training takes place as stated in the human resource plan. Unplanned training takes place as a result of observation, conversation, and project performance appraisals conducted during the controlling process of managing the project team.

130. Answer: C.
PMBOK® Guide, page 235, Section 9.3.3.1

Team Performance Assessments
As project team development efforts such as training, team building, and co-location are implemented, the project management team makes formal or informal assessments of the project team's effectiveness. Effective team development strategies and activities are expected to increase the team's performance, which increases the likelihood of meeting project objectives. . ..

The evaluation of a team's effectiveness may include indicators such as:
* Improvements in skills that allow individuals to perform assignments more effectively,
* Improvements in competencies that help the team perform better as a team,
* Reduced staff turnover rate, and
* Increased team cohesiveness where team members share information and experiences openly and help each other to improve the overall project performance.

131. Answer: B.
PMBOK® Guide, pages 227–228, Section 9.2.2.2; and Appendix G, Section G.8

Negotiation
Staff assignments are negotiated on many projects. For example, the project management team may need to negotiate with:
- Functional managers to ensure that the project receives appropriately competent staff in the required time frame, and that the project team members will be able, willing, and authorized to work on the project until their responsibilities are completed,
- Other project management teams within the performing organization to appropriately assign scarce or specialized human resources, and
- External organizations, vendors, suppliers, contractors, etc., for appropriate, scarce, specialized, qualified, certified, or other such specified human resources. Special consideration should be given to external negotiating policies, practices, processes, guidelines, legal, and other such criteria.

The project management team's ability to influence others plays an important role in negotiating staff assignments, as do the politics of the organizations involved. . .

Negotiation
Negotiation is a strategy of conferring with parties of shared or opposed interests with a view to compromise or reach an agreement. Negotiation is an integral part of project management and done well, increases the probability of project success.

132. Answer: C.
PMBOK® Guide, page 223, Section 9.1.3.1

Staffing management plan. The staffing management plan, a part of the human resources plan within the project management plan, describes when and how human resource requirements will be met. . .
○ *Staff acquisition.* A number of questions arise when planning the acquisition of project team members. For example, will the human resources come from within the organization or from external, contracted sources? Will team members need to work in a central location or can they work from distant locations? What are the costs associated with each level of expertise needed for the project? How much assistance can the organization's human resource department and functional managers provide to the project management team?

133. Answer: C.
PMBOK® Guide, pages 239–240, Section 9.4.2.3

Conflict Management
There are six general techniques for resolving conflict. As each one has its place and use, these are not given in any particular order:
• **Withdrawing/Avoiding.** Retreating from an actual or potential conflict situation.
• **Smoothing/Accommodating.** Emphasizing areas of agreement rather than areas of difference.
• **Compromising.** Searching for solutions that bring some degree of satisfaction to all parties.
• **Forcing.** Pushing one's viewpoint at the expense of others; offers only win-lose solutions.
• **Collaborating.** Incorporating multiple viewpoints and insights from differing perspectives; leads to consensus and commitment.
• **Confronting/Problem Solving.** Treating conflict as a problem to be solved by examining alternatives; requires a give-and-take attitude and open dialogue.

Project Communications Management
(Chapter 10 of the *PMBOK® Guide*)

134. Answer: A.
PMBOK® Guide, page 243, Introduction; and page 244, Figure 10-1

Project Communications Management
Figure 10-1 provides an overview of the Project Communications Management processes which include the following:

10.1 Identify Stakeholders—The process of identifying all people or organizations impacted by the project, and documenting relevant information regarding their interests, involvement, and impact on project success.

10.2 Plan Communications—The process of determining the project stakeholder information needs and defining a communication approach.

10.3 Distribute Information—The process of making relevant information available to project stakeholders as planned.

10.4 Manage Stakeholder Expectations—The process of communicating and working with stakeholders to meet their needs and addressing issues as they occur.

10.5 Report Performance—The process of collecting and distributing performance information, including status reports, progress measurements, and forecasts.

135. Answer: A.
PMBOK® Guide, page 253, Section 10.2.1; and page 252, Figure 10-6

Plan Communications: Inputs
.1 Stakeholder Register
.2 Stakeholder Management Strategy
.3 Enterprise Environmental Factors
.4 Organizational Process Assets

136. Answer: D.
PMBOK® Guide, pages 256–257, Section 10.2.3.1

Communications Management Plan
The communications management plan usually provides:
- Stakeholder communication requirements;
- Information to be communicated, including language, format, content, and level of detail;
- Reason for the distribution of that information;
- Time frame and frequency for the distribution of required information;
- Person responsible for communicating the information;
- Person responsible for authorizing release of confidential information;
- Person or groups who will receive the information;
- Methods or technologies used to convey the information, such as memos, e-mail, and/or press releases;
- Resources allocated for communication activities, including time and budget;
- Escalation process identifying time frames and the management chain (names) for escalation of issues that cannot be resolved at a lower staff level;
- Method for updating and refining the communications management plan as the project progresses and develops;
- Glossary of common terminology;
- Flow charts of the information flow in the project, workflows with possible sequence of authorization, list of reports, and meeting plans, etc.; and
- Communication constraints, usually derived from specific legislation or regulation, technology, and organizational policies, etc.

137. Answer: C.
PMBOK® Guide, page 260, Section 10.3.2.2

Information Distribution Tools
Project information can be distributed using a variety of tools, including:
- Hard-copy document distribution, manual filing systems, press releases, and shared-access electronic databases;
- Electronic communication and conferencing tools, such as e-mail, fax, voice mail, telephone, video and web conferencing, websites and web publishing; and
- Electronic tools for project management, such as web interfaces to scheduling and project management software, meeting and virtual office support software, portals, and collaborative work management tools.

138. Answer: C.
PMBOK® Guide, page 254, Section 10.2.2.2

Communication Technology
The methods used to transfer information among project stakeholders can vary significantly. . .

Factors that can affect the project include:
- **Urgency of the need for information**. . .
- **Availability of technology**. . .
- **Expected project staffing**. . .
- **Duration of the project**. . .
- **Project environment**. . .

139. Answer: B.
PMBOK® Guide, pages 268–270, Section 10.5.2; and page 266, Figure 10-13

Report Performance: Tools and Techniques
.1 Variance Analysis
.2 Forecasting Methods
.3 Communication Methods
.4 Reporting Systems

140. Answer: B.
PMBOK® Guide, page 255, Section 10.2.2.3 and Figure 10-8

Communication Models
The components in the communications model need to be taken into account when discussing project communications. As part of the communications process, the sender is responsible for making the information clear and complete so that the receiver can receive it correctly, and for confirming that it is properly understood. The receiver is responsible for making sure that the information is received in its entirety, understood correctly, and acknowledged. A failure in communication can negatively impact the project.

141. Answer: C.

PMBOK® Guide, page 255, Section 10.2.2.3 and Figure 10-8; and Appendix G, Section G.4

Communication Models

The components in the communications model need to be taken into account when discussing project communications. As part of the communications process, the sender is responsible for making the information clear and complete so that the receiver can receive it correctly, and for confirming that it is properly understood. The receiver is responsible for making sure that the information is received in its entirety, understood correctly, and acknowledged. A failure in communication can negatively impact the project.

Communication

Listening is an important part of communication. Listening techniques, both active and effective give the user insight to problem areas, negotiation and conflict management strategies, decision making, and problem resolution.

142. Answer: D.

PMBOK® Guide, pages 253–254, Section 10.1.2.1

Communication Requirements Analysis

Information typically used to determine project communication requirements includes:
- Organization charts,
- Project organization and stakeholder responsibility relationships,
- Disciplines, departments, and specialties involved in the project,
- Logistics of how many persons will be involved with the project and at which locations,
- Internal information needs (e.g., communicating across organizations),
- External information needs (e.g., communicating with the media, public, or contractors), and
- Stakeholder information from the stakeholder register and the stakeholder management strategy.

143. Answer: A.

PMBOK® Guide, page 266, Section 10.5

Report Performance

Report Performance is the process of collecting and distributing performance information, including status reports, progress measurements, and forecasts. See Figures 10-13 and 10-14. The performance reporting process involves the periodic collection and analysis of baseline versus actual data to understand and communicate the project progress and performance as well as to forecast the project results.

Performance reports need to provide information at an appropriate level for each audience. The format may range from a simple status report to more elaborate reports. A simple status report might show performance information, such as percent complete, or status dashboards for each area (i.e., scope, schedule, cost, and quality).

144. Answer: C.

PMBOK® Guide, page 245, Introduction; and page 244, Figure 10-1

Project Communications Management

Communication activity has many potential dimensions, including:

- Internal (within the project) and external (customer, other projects, the media, the public),
- Formal (reports, memos, briefings) and informal (emails, ad-hoc discussions),
- Vertical (up and down the organization) and horizontal (with peers),
- Official (newsletters, annual report) and unofficial (off the record communications),
- Written and oral, and
- Verbal and non-verbal (voice inflections, body language).

145. Answer: C.

PMBOK® Guide, page 260, Section 10.3.2.3

Information Distribution Tools

Project information can be distributed using a variety of tools, including:

- Hard-copy document distribution, manual filing systems, press releases, and shared-access electronic databases;
- Electronic communication and conferencing tools, such as e-mail, fax, voice mail, telephone, video and web conferencing, websites and web publishing; and
- Electronic tools for project management, such as web interfaces to scheduling and project management software, meeting and virtual office support software, portals, and collaborative work management tools.

146. Answer: A.
PMBOK® Guide, page 253, Section 10.1.2.1

Communication Requirements Analysis
The project manager should also consider the number of potential communication channels or paths as an indicator of the complexity of a project's communications. The total number of potential communication channels is $n(n-1)/2$, where n represents the number of stakeholders. Thus, a project with 10 stakeholders has $10(10-1)/2 = 45$ potential communication channels. A key component of planning the project's actual communications, therefore, is to determine and limit who will communicate with whom and who will receive what information.

147. Answer: B.
PMBOK® Guide, page 261, Section 10.3.3.1

Lessons learned documentation. Documentation includes the causes of issues, reasoning behind the corrective action chosen, and other types of lessons learned about information distribution. Lessons learned are documented and distributed so that they become part of the historical database for both the project and the performing organization.

Project Risk Management
(Chapter 11 of the PMBOK® Guide)

148. Answer: D.
PMBOK® Guide, page 273, Introduction; and page 274, Figure 11-1

Project Risk Management
Project Risk Management includes the processes of conducting risk management planning, identification, analysis, response planning, and monitoring and control on a project. The objectives of Project Risk Management are to increase the probability and impact of positive events, and decrease the probability and impact of negative events in the project.

Figure 11-1 provides an overview of Project Risk Management processes, which are as follows:

11.1 Plan Risk Management—The process of defining how to conduct risk management activities for a project.

11.2 Identify Risks—The process of determining which risks may affect the project and documenting their characteristics.

11.3 Perform Qualitative Risk Analysis—The process of prioritizing risks for further analysis or action by assessing and combining their probability of occurrence and impact.

11.4 Perform Quantitative Risk Analysis—The process of numerically analyzing the effect of identified risks on overall project objectives.

11.5 Plan Risk Responses—The process of developing options and actions to enhance opportunities and to reduce threats to project objectives.

11.6 Monitor and Control Risks—The process of implementing risk response plans, tracking identified risks, monitoring residual risks, identifying new risks, and evaluating risk process effectiveness throughout the project.

149. Answer: A.

PMBOK® Guide, page 303, Section 11.5.2.1

Strategies for Negative Risks or Threats

Three of the following strategies typically deal with threats or risks that may have negative impacts on project objectives if they occur. The fourth strategy, accept, can be used for negative risks or threats as well as positive risks or opportunities. These strategies, described below, are to avoid, transfer, mitigate, or accept.

150. Answer: D.

PMBOK® Guide, page 303, Section 11.5.2.1

Transfer. Risk transfer requires shifting some or all of the negative impact of a threat, along with ownership of the response, to a third party. Transferring the risk simply gives another party responsibility for its management—it does not eliminate it. Transferring liability for risk is most effective in dealing with financial risk exposure. Risk transference nearly always involves payment of a risk premium to the party taking on the risk. Transference tools can be quite diverse and include, but are not limited to, the use of insurance, performance bonds, warranties, guarantees, etc. Contracts may be used to transfer liability for specified risks to another party. For example, when a buyer has capabilities that the seller does not possess, it may be prudent to transfer some work and its concurrent risk contractually back to the buyer. In many cases, use of a cost-plus contract may transfer the cost risk to the buyer, while a fixed-price contract may transfer risk to the seller.

151. Answer: B.
PMBOK® Guide, page 276, Introduction

Project Risk Management
To be successful, the organization should be committed to address risk management proactively and consistently throughout the project. A conscious choice must be made at all levels of the organization to actively identify and pursue effective risk management during the life of the project. Risk exists the moment a project is conceived. Moving forward on a project without a proactive focus on risk management increases the impact that a realized risk can have on the project and can potentially lead to project failure.

152. Answer: C.
PMBOK® Guide, pages 303–305, Section 11.5.2.1 and Section 11.5.2.2

.1 Strategies for Negative Risks or Threats
- **Accept.** This strategy is adopted because it is seldom possible to eliminate all threats from a project. This strategy indicates that the project team has decided not to change the project management plan to deal with a risk, or is unable to identify any other suitable response strategy. This strategy can be either passive or active. Passive acceptance requires no action except to document the strategy, leaving the project team to deal with the risks as they occur. The most common active acceptance strategy is to establish a contingency reserve, including amounts of time, money, or resources to handle the risks.

.2 Strategies for Positive Risks or Opportunities
- **Accept.** Accepting an opportunity is being willing to take advantage of it if it comes along, but not actively pursuing it.

153. Answer: A.
PMBOK® Guide, page 288, Section 11.2.3; and page 282, Figure 11-6

> **Identify Risks: Outputs**
> The main outputs from Identify Risks are typically contained in the risk register.
> **.1 Risk Register**

154. Answer: A.
PMBOK® Guide, page 287, Section 11.2.2.3

> **Checklist Analysis**
> Risk identification checklists can be developed based on historical information and knowledge that has been accumulated from previous similar projects and from other sources of information. The lowest level of the RBS can also be used as a risk checklist. While a checklist can be quick and simple, it is impossible to build an exhaustive one. The team should make sure to explore items that do not appear on the checklist. The checklist should be reviewed during project closure to incorporate new lessons learned and improve it for use on future projects.

155. Answer: C.
PMBOK® Guide, pages 284–286, Section 11.2.1; and page 282, Figure 11-6

> **Identify Risks: Inputs**
> **.1 Risk Management Plan**
> **.2 Activity Cost Estimates**
> **.3 Activity Duration Estimates**
> **.4 Scope Baseline**
> **.5 Stakeholder Register**
> **.6 Cost Management Plan**
> **.7 Schedule Management Plan**
> **.8 Quality Management Plan**
> **.9 Project Documents**
> **.10 Enterprise Environmental Factors**
> **.11 Organizational Process Assets**

156. Answer: B.
PMBOK® Guide, pages 305–307, Section 11.5.3; and page 302, Figure 11-17

Plan Risk Responses: Outputs
.1 Risk Register Updates
.2 Risk-Related Contract Decisions
.3 Project Management Plan Updates
.4 Project Document Updates

157. Answer: D.
PMBOK® Guide, pages 296–300, Section 11.4.2; and page 295, Figure 11-11

Perform Quantitative Risk Analysis: Tools and Techniques
.1 Data Gathering and Representation Techniques
.2 Quantitative Risk Analysis and Modeling Techniques
.3 Expert Judgment

158. Answer: A.
PMBOK® Guide, pages 300–301, Section 11.4.3; and page 295, Figure 11-11

Perform Quantitative Risk Analysis: Outputs
.1 Risk Register Updates
The risk register is further updated to include a quantitative risk report detailing quantitative approaches, outputs, and recommendations. Updates include the following main components:
• **Probabilistic analysis of the project.**
• **Probability of achieving cost and time objectives.**
• **Prioritized list of quantified risks.**
• **Trends in quantitative risk analysis results.**

159. Answer: D.

PMBOK ® Guide, page 281, Section 11.1.3.1 and Figure 11-5; and page 291, Section 11.3.2.2

Definitions of risk probability and impact. The quality and credibility of the Perform Qualitative Risk Analysis process requires that different levels of the risks' probabilities and impacts be defined. . . Figure 11-5 is an example of definitions of negative impacts that could be used in evaluating risk impacts related to four project objectives. (Similar tables could be established with a positive impact perspective). The figure illustrates both relative and numeric (in this case, nonlinear) approaches.

Risk Probability and Impact Assessment
Risk probability assessment investigates the likelihood that each specific risk will occur. Risk impact assessment investigates the potential effect on a project objective such as schedule, cost, quality, or performance, including both negative effects for threats and positive effects for opportunities.

Probability and Impact Matrix
Risks can be prioritized for further quantitative analysis and response based on their risk rating. Usually, these risk-rating rules are specified by the organization in advance of the project and included in organizational process assets. Risk-rating rules can be tailored to the specific project in the Plan Risk Management process (Section 11.1). Evaluation of each risk's importance and, hence, priority for attention, is typically conducted using a look-up table or a probability and impact matrix (Figure 11-10). Such a matrix specifies combinations of probability and impact that lead to rating the risks as low, moderate, or high priority.

160. Answer: B.

PMBOK® Guide, pages 311–312, Section 11.6.3; and page 308, Figure 11-19

> **Monitor and Control Risks: Outputs**
> .1 Risk Register Updates
> .2 Organizational Process Assets Updates
> .3 Change Requests
> .4 Project Management Plan Updates
> .5 Project Document Updates

161. Answer: D.

PMBOK® Guide, page 286, Section 11.2.2.2

> **Delphi technique.** The Delphi technique is a way to reach a consensus of experts. Project risk experts participate in this technique anonymously. A facilitator uses a questionnaire to solicit ideas about the important project risks. The responses are summarized and are then recirculated to the experts for further comment. Consensus may be reached in a few rounds of this process. The Delphi technique helps reduce bias in the data and keeps any one person from having undue influence on the outcome.

162. Answer: A.
PMBOK® Guide, pages 291–292, Section 11.3.2.2 and Figure 11-10

Probability and Impact Matrix

Risks can be prioritized for further quantitative analysis and response based on their risk rating. Usually, these risk-rating rules are specified by the organization in advance of the project and included in organizational process assets. Risk-rating rules can be tailored to the specific project in the Plan Risk Management process (Section 11.1). Evaluation of each risk's importance and, hence, priority for attention, is typically conducted using a look-up table or a probability and impact matrix (Figure 11-10). Such a matrix specifies combinations of probability and impact that lead to rating the risks as low, moderate, or high priority. The dark gray area (with the largest numbers) represents high risk, the medium gray area (with the smallest numbers) represents low risk, and the light gray area (with in-between numbers) represents moderate risk

As illustrated in Figure 11-5, an organization can rate a risk separately for each objective (e.g., cost, time, and scope). In addition, it can develop ways to determine one overall rating for each risk. An overall project rating scheme can be developed to reflect the organization's preference for one objective over another and using those preferences to develop a weighting of the risks that are assessed by objective. Finally, opportunities and threats can be handled in the same matrix using definitions of the different levels of impact that are appropriate for each.

The risk rating helps guide risk responses. For example, risks that have a negative impact on objectives if they occur (threats), and that are in the high-risk (dark gray) zone of the matrix, may require priority action and aggressive response strategies. Threats in the low-risk (medium gray) zone may not require proactive management action beyond being placed on a watchlist or adding a contingency reserve.

163. Answer: B.

PMBOK® Guide, page 298, Section 11.4.2.2

Sensitivity analysis. Sensitivity analysis helps to determine which risks have the most potential impact on the project. It examines the extent to which the uncertainty of each project element affects the objective being examined when all other uncertain elements are held at their baseline values. One typical display of sensitivity analysis is the tornado diagram, which is useful for comparing relative importance and impact of variables that have a high degree of uncertainty to those that are more stable.

164. Answer: C.

PMBOK® Guide, page 297, Section 11.4.2.1; page 298, Section 11.4.2.2; page 299, Figure 11-15; page 303, Section 11.5.2; and Glossary

Probability distributions. Continuous probability distributions, used extensively in modeling and simulation (Section 11.4.2.2) represent the uncertainty in values such as durations of schedule activities and costs of project components. Discrete distributions can be used to represent uncertain events such as the outcome of a test or a possible scenario in a decision tree.

Expected monetary value analysis. Expected monetary value (EMV) analysis is a statistical concept that calculates the average outcome when the future includes scenarios that may or may not happen (i.e., analysis under uncertainty). The EMV of opportunities will generally be expressed as positive values, while those of threats will be negative. EMV requires a risk-neutral assumption, neither risk averse, nor risk seeking. EMV for a project is calculated by multiplying the value of each possible outcome by its probability of occurrence and adding the products together. A common use of this type of analysis is in decision tree analysis (Figure 11-15).

Plan Risk Responses: Tools and Techniques

Several risk response strategies are available. The strategy or mix of strategies most likely to be effective should be selected for each risk. Risk analysis tools, such as decision tree analysis (Section 11.4.2.2), can be used to choose the most appropriate responses.

Decision Tree Analysis [Technique]. The decision tree is a diagram that describes a decision under consideration and the implications of choosing one or another of the available alternatives. It is used when some future scenarios or outcomes of actions are uncertain. It incorporates probabilities and the costs or rewards of each logical path of events and future decisions, and uses expected monetary value analysis to help the organization identify the relative values of alternate actions. See also *expected monetary value analysis.*

165. Answer: C.

PMBOK® Guide, pages 279–282, Section 11.1.3.1

Risk Management Plan

The risk management plan describes how risk management will be structured and performed on the project. It becomes a subset of the project management plan (Section 4.2.3.1). The risk management plan includes the following:
- **Methodology.**
- **Roles and responsibilities.**
- **Budgeting.**
- **Timing.**
- **Risk categories.**
- **Definitions of risk probability and impact.**
- **Probability and impact matrix.**
- **Revised stakeholders' tolerances.**
- **Reporting formats.**
- **Tracking.**

166. Answer: C.
PMBOK® Guide, page 289, Section 11.3

Perform Qualitative Risk Analysis
Perform Qualitative Risk Analysis is the process of prioritizing risks for further analysis or action by assessing and combining their probability of occurrence and impact (see Figures 11-8 and 11-9). Organizations can improve the project's performance by focusing on high-priority risks. Perform Qualitative Risk Analysis assesses the priority of identified risks using their relative probability or likelihood of occurrence, the corresponding impact on project objectives if the risks occur, as well as other factors such as the time frame for response and the organization's risk tolerance associated with the project constraints of cost, schedule, scope, and quality.

167. Answer: A.
PMBOK® Guide, pages 311, Section 11.6.3.1

Risk Register Updates
An updated risk register includes, but is not limited to:
- Outcomes of risk reassessments, risk audits, and periodic risk reviews. These outcomes may include identification of new risk events, updates to probability, impact, priority, response plans, ownership, and other elements of the risk register. Outcomes can also include closing risks that are no longer applicable and releasing their associated reserves.
- Actual outcomes of the project's risks and of the risk responses. This information can help project managers to plan for risk throughout their organizations, as well as on future projects.

168. Answer: C.

PMBOK® Guide, page 298, Section 11.4.2.2

Expected monetary value analysis. Expected monetary value (EMV) analysis is a statistical concept that calculates the average outcome when the future includes scenarios that may or may not happen (i.e., analysis under uncertainty). The EMV of opportunities will generally be expressed as positive values, while those of threats will be negative. EMV requires a risk-neutral assumption, neither risk averse, nor risk seeking. EMV for a project is calculated by multiplying the value of each possible outcome by its probability of occurrence and adding the products together. A common use of this type of analysis is in decision tree analysis (Figure 11-15).

Project Procurement Management
(Chapter 12 of the PMBOK® Guide)

169. Answer: C.
PMBOK® Guide, pages 319–321, Section 12.1.1; and page 317, Figure 12-2

Plan Procurements: Inputs
.1 Scope Baseline
.2 Requirements Documentation
.3 Teaming Agreements
.4 Risk Register
.5 Risk-Related Contract Decisions
.6 Activity Resource Requirements
.7 Project Schedule
.8 Activity Cost Estimates
.9 Cost Performance Baseline
.10 Enterprise Environmental Factors
.11 Organizational Process Assets

170. Answer: C.
PMBOK® Guide, page 326, Section 12.1.3.4

Procurement Documents
Procurement documents are used to solicit proposals from prospective sellers. Terms such as bid, tender, or quotation are generally used when the seller selection decision will be based on price (as when buying commercial or standard items), while a term such as proposal is generally used when other considerations, such as technical capability or technical approach are paramount. Common terms are in use for different types of procurement documents and may include request for information (RFI), invitation for bid (IFB), request for proposal (RFP), request for quotation (RFQ), tender notice, invitation for negotiation, and invitation for seller's initial response. Specific procurement terminology used may vary by industry and location of the procurement.

171. Answer: D.
PMBOK® Guide, page 326, Section 12.1.3.4

Procurement Documents
The buyer structures procurement documents to facilitate an accurate and complete response from each prospective seller and to facilitate easy evaluation of the responses. These documents include a description of the desired form of the response, the relevant procurement statement of work (SOW) and any required contractual provisions. With government contracting, some or all of the content and structure of procurement documents can be defined by regulation.

172. Answer: C.
PMBOK® Guide, page 338, Section 12.3.1.5

Approved Change Requests
Approved change requests can include modifications to the terms and conditions of the contract including the procurement statement of work, pricing, and description of the products, services, or results to be provided. All changes are formally documented in writing and approved before being implemented.

173. Answer: C.
PMBOK® Guide, page 332, Section 12.2.2.5

Advertising
Existing lists of potential sellers can often be expanded by placing advertisements in general circulation publications such as selected newspapers or in specialty trade publications. Some government jurisdictions require public advertising of certain types of procurement items, and most government jurisdictions require public advertising of pending government contracts.

174. Answer: C.
PMBOK® Guide, page 339, Section 12.3.2.5

Payment Systems
Payments to the seller are typically processed by the
accounts payable system of the buyer after certification
of satisfactory work by an authorized person on the
project team. All payments should be made and
documented in strict accordance with the terms of the
contract.

175. Answer: A.
PMBOK® Guide, page 344, Section 12.4.3.2

Deliverable acceptance. The buyer, usually through
its authorized procurement administrator, provides the
seller with formal written notice that the deliverables
have been accepted or rejected. Requirements for
formal deliverable acceptance, and how to address
non-conforming deliverables, are usually defined in the
contract.

176. Answer: B.
PMBOK® Guide, page 322, Section 12.1.2.3

Fixed-price contracts. This category of contracts
involves setting a fixed total price for a defined product
or service to be provided. Fixed-price contracts may
also incorporate financial incentives for achieving or
exceeding selected project objectives, such as schedule
delivery dates, cost and technical performance, or
anything that can be quantified and subsequently
measured. Sellers under fixed-price contracts are legally
obligated to complete such contracts, with possible
financial damages if they do not. Under the fixed-price
arrangement, buyers must precisely specify the product
or services being procured. Changes in scope can be
accommodated, but generally at an increase in contract
price.

177. Answer: D.
PMBOK® Guide, page 339, Section 12.3.2.6

Claims Administration
Contested changes and potential constructive changes are those requested changes where the buyer and seller cannot reach an agreement on compensation for the change, or cannot agree that a change has occurred. These contested changes are variously called claims, disputes, or appeals. Claims are documented, processed, monitored, and managed throughout the contract life cycle, usually in accordance with the terms of the contract. If the parties themselves do not resolve a claim, it may have to be handled in accordance with alternative dispute resolution (ADR) typically following procedures established in the contract. Settlement of all claims and disputes through negotiation is the preferred method.

178. Answer: C.
PMBOK® Guide, page 341, Section 12.3.3.3

Change Requests
Requested but unresolved changes can include direction provided by the buyer, or actions taken by the seller, that the other party considers a constructive change to the contract. Since any of these constructive changes may be disputed by one party and can lead to a claim against the other party, such changes are uniquely identified and documented by project correspondence.

179. Answer: A.
PMBOK® Guide, page 343, Section 12.4.2.1

Procurement Audits
A procurement audit is a structured review of the procurement process originating from the Plan Procurements process (Section 12.1) through Administer Procurements (Section 12.3). The objective of a procurement audit is to identify successes and failures that warrant recognition in the preparation or administration of other procurement contracts on the project, or on other projects within the performing organization.

180. Answer: A.
PMBOK® Guide, pages 322–324, Section 12.1.2.3

Contract Types
The risk shared between the buyer and seller is determined by the contract type. Although the firm-fixed-price type of contractual arrangement is typically the preferred type which is encouraged and often demanded by most organizations, there are times when another contract form may be in the best interests of the project. If a contract type other than fixed-price is intended, it is incumbent on the project team to justify its use. The type of contract to be used and the specific contract terms and conditions fix the degree of risk being assumed by the buyer and seller.

All legal contractual relationships generally fall into one of two broad families, either fixed-price or cost reimbursable. Also, there is a third hybrid-type commonly in use called the time and materials contract. The more popular of the contract types in use are discussed below as discrete types, but in practice it is not unusual to combine one or more types into a single procurement.
- **Fixed-price contracts.**
- **Cost-reimbursable contracts.**
- **Time and Material Contracts (T&M).**

181. Answer: B.
PMBOK® Guide, pages 325–326, Section 12.1.3.2

Procurement Statements of Work
The statement of work (SOW) for each procurement is developed from the project scope baseline and defines only that portion of the project scope that is to be included within the related contract. The procurement SOW describes the procurement item in sufficient detail to allow prospective sellers to determine if they are capable of providing the products, services, or results. Sufficient detail can vary based on the nature of the item, the needs of the buyer, or the expected contract form. Information included in a SOW can include specifications, quantity desired, quality levels, performance data, period of performance, work location, and other requirements.

The procurement SOW is written to be clear, complete, and concise. It includes a description of any collateral services required, such as performance reporting or post-project operational support for the procured item. In some application areas, there are specific content and format requirements for a procurement SOW. Each individual procurement item requires a SOW. However, multiple products or services can be grouped as one procurement item within a single SOW.

The procurement SOW can be revised and refined as required as it moves through the procurement process until incorporated into a signed contract award.

182. Answer: C.

PMBOK® Guide, page 344, Section 12.4.3; page 342, Figure 12-8; and Glossary

Close Procurements: Outputs
.1 Closed Procurements
.2 Organizational Process Assets Updates
 • Procurement file.
 • **Deliverable acceptance.** The buyer, usually through its authorized procurement administrator, provides the seller with formal written notice that the deliverables have been accepted or rejected. . .
 • **Lessons learned documentation.**

Request for Proposal (RFP). A type of procurement document used to request proposals from prospective sellers of products or services. In some application areas, it may have a narrower or more specific meaning.

Request for Quotation (RFQ). A type of procurement document used to request price quotations from prospective sellers of common or standard products or services. Sometimes used in place of request for proposal and in some application areas, it may have a narrower or more specific meaning.

183. Answer: D.

PMBOK® Guide, page 327, Section 12.1.3.5

Source Selection Criteria
Selection criteria are often included as a part of the procurement documents. Such criteria are developed and used to rate or score seller proposals, and can be objective or subjective.

Selection criteria can be limited to purchase price if the procurement item is readily available from a number of acceptable sellers. Purchase price in this context includes both the cost of the item and all ancillary expenses such as delivery.

184. Answer: D.
PMBOK® Guide, pages 331–333, Section 12.2.2; and page 329, Figure 12-4

> **Conduct Procurements: Tools and Techniques**
> **.1 Bidder Conferences**
> **.2 Proposal Evaluation Techniques**
> **.3 Independent Estimates**
> **.4 Expert Judgment**
> **.5 Advertising**
> **.6 Internet Search**
> **.7 Procurement Negotiations**

185. Answer: B.
PMBOK® Guide, page 323, Section 12.1.2.3

> **Cost Plus Fixed Fee Contracts (CPFF).** The seller is reimbursed for all allowable costs for performing the contract work, and receives a fixed fee payment calculated as a percentage of the initial estimated project costs. Fee is paid only for completed work and does not change due to seller performance. Fee amounts do not change unless the project scope changes.

Glossary

186. Answer: B.
PMBOK® Guide Glossary; and page 304, Section 11.5.2.1

> **Acceptance Criteria.** Those criteria, including performance requirements and essential conditions, which must be met before project deliverables are accepted.

> **Accept.** . . .This strategy can be either passive or active. Passive acceptance requires no action except to document the strategy, leaving the project team to deal with the risks as they occur. The most common active acceptance strategy is to establish a contingency reserve, including amounts of time, money, or resources to handle the risks.

187. Answer: C.
PMBOK® Guide Glossary

> **Baseline.** An approved plan for a project, plus or minus approved changes. It is compared to actual performance to determine if performance is within acceptable variance thresholds. Generally refers to the current baseline, but may refer to the original or some other baseline. Usually used with a modifier (e.g., cost performance baseline, schedule baseline, performance measurement baseline, technical baseline).

188. Answer: A.
PMBOK® Guide Glossary

> **Code of Accounts** [Tool]. Any numbering system used to uniquely identify each component of the work breakdown structure.

189. Answer: D.
PMBOK® Guide Glossary

Stakeholder. Person or organization (e.g., customer, sponsor, performing organization, or the public) that is actively involved in the project, or whose interests may be positively or negatively affected by execution or completion of the project. A stakeholder may also exert influence over the project and its deliverables.

190. Answer: C.
PMBOK® Guide Glossary

Scope Management Plan [Output/Input]. The document that describes how the project scope will be defined, developed, and verified and how the work breakdown structure will be created and defined, and that provides guidance on how the project scope will be managed and controlled by the project management team. It is contained in or is a subsidiary plan of the project management plan.

191. Answer: A.
PMBOK® Guide Glossary

Project Scope Statement [Output/Input]. The narrative description of the project scope, including major deliverables, project assumptions, project constraints, and a description of work, that provides a documented basis for making future project decisions and for confirming or developing a common understanding of project scope among the stakeholders.

192. Answer: B.
PMBOK® Guide Glossary; and page 121, Section 5.3.3.1

Work Package. A deliverable or project work component at the lowest level of each branch of the work breakdown structure. See also *control account*.

Control Account [Tool]. A management control point where scope, budget (resource plans), actual cost, and schedule are integrated and compared to earned value for performance measurement. See also *work package*.

WBS
. . . A control account is a management control point where scope, cost, and schedule are integrated and compared to the earned value for performance measurement. Control accounts are placed at selected management points in the WBS. Each control account may include one or more work packages, but each of the work packages must be associated with only one control account.

193. Answer: C.
PMBOK® Guide Glossary

Float. Also called slack. See *total float* and *free float*.

Free Float. The amount of time that a schedule activity can be delayed without delaying the early start date of any immediately following schedule activities. See also *total float*.

Total Float. The total amount of time that a schedule activity may be delayed from its early start date without delaying the project finish date, or violating a schedule constraint. Calculated using the critical path method technique and determining the difference between the early finish dates and late finish dates. See also *free float*.

194. Answer: A.
PMBOK® Guide Glossary

Performance Measurement Baseline. An approved integrated scope-schedule-cost plan for the project work against which project execution is compared to measure and manage performance. Technical and quality parameters may also be included.

195. Answer: C.
PMBOK® Guide Glossary

Cost of Quality (COQ) [Technique]. A method of determining the costs incurred to ensure quality. Prevention and appraisal costs (cost of conformance) include costs for quality planning, quality control (QC), and quality assurance to ensure compliance to requirements (i.e., training, QC systems, etc.). Failure costs (cost of non-conformance) include costs to rework products, components, or processes that are non-compliant, costs of warranty work and waste, and loss of reputation.

196. Answer: B.
PMBOK® Guide Glossary

Common Acronyms
FFP   firm fixed price

Firm-Fixed-Price (FFP) Contract. A type of fixed price contract where the buyer pays the seller a set amount (as defined by the contract), regardless of the seller's costs.

197. Answer: B.

PMBOK® Guide Glossary; page 82, Section 4.2.3.1; and page 93, Section 4.5

> **Baseline.** An approved plan for a project, plus or minus approved changes. It is compared to actual performance to determine if performance is within acceptable variance thresholds. Generally refers to the current baseline, but may refer to the original or some other baseline. Usually used with a modifier (e.g., cost performance baseline, schedule baseline, performance measurement baseline, technical baseline).

> . . . Once the project management plan is baselined, it may only be changed when a change request is generated and approved through the Perform Integrated Change Control process.

> . . . The project management plan, the project scope statement, and other deliverables are maintained by carefully and continuously managing changes, either by rejecting changes or by approving changes thereby assuring that only approved changes are incorporated into a revised baseline.

198. Answer: D.

PMBOK® Guide Glossary

> **Product Life Cycle.** A collection of generally sequential, non-overlapping product phases whose name and number are determined by the manufacturing and control needs of the organization. The last product life cycle phase for a product is generally the product's retirement. Generally, a project life cycle is contained within one or more product life cycles.

199. Answer: C.
PMBOK® Guide Glossary

Performance Measurement Baseline. An approved integrated scope-schedule-cost plan for the project work against which project execution is compared to measure and manage performance. Technical and quality parameters may also be included.

200. Answer: A.
PMBOK® Guide Glossary

Workaround [Technique]. A response to a negative risk that has occurred. Distinguished from contingency plan in that a workaround is not planned in advance of the occurrence of the risk event.

Appendix G
(Interpersonal Skills)

201. Answer: D.
PMBOK® Guide Appendix G, Section G.1; and page 240,
Section 9.4.2.5

Leadership
Leadership involves focusing the efforts of a group of
people toward a common goal and enabling them to
work as a team. In general terms, leadership is the
ability to get things done through others. Respect and
trust, rather than fear and submission, are the key
elements of effective leadership. Although important
throughout all project phases, effective leadership is
critical during the beginning phases of a project when
the emphasis is on communicating the vision and
motivating and inspiring project participants to achieve
high performance.

Leadership. Successful projects require strong
leadership skills. Leadership is important through all
phases of the project life cycle. It is especially
important to communicate the vision and inspire the
project team to achieve high performance.

202. Answer: B.

PMBOK® Guide Appendix G, Section G.2; and page 232, Section 9.3.2.3

Team Building

Team building is the process of helping a group of individuals, bound by a common sense of purpose, to work interdependently with each other, the leader, external stakeholders, and the organization. The result of good leadership and good team building is teamwork.

Team-building activities consist of tasks (establish goals, define, and negotiate roles and procedures) and processes (interpersonal behavior with emphasis on communication, conflict management, motivation, and leadership). Developing a team environment involves handling project team problems and discussing these as team issues without placing blame on individuals. Team building can be further enhanced by obtaining top management support, encouraging team member commitment, introducing appropriate rewards, recognition and ethics, creating a team identity, managing conflicts effectively, promoting trust and open communication among team members, and providing leadership.

Team-Building Activities

One of the most important skills in developing a team environment involves handling project team problems and discussing these as team issues. The entire team should be encouraged to work collaboratively to resolve these issues. To build effective project teams, project managers should obtain top management support, obtain commitment of team members, introduce appropriate rewards and recognition, create a team identity, manage conflicts effectively, promote trust and open communication among team members, and, above all, provide good team leadership.

203. Answer: C.

PMBOK® Guide Appendix G, Section G.3; and page 234, Section 9.3.2.6

Motivation

Motivating in a project environment involves creating an environment to meet project objectives while offering maximum self-satisfaction related to what people value most. These values may include job satisfaction, challenging work, a sense of accomplishment, achievement and growth, sufficient financial compensation, and other rewards and recognition the individual considers necessary and important.

Recognition and Rewards

People are motivated if they feel they are valued in the organization and this value is demonstrated by the rewards given to them. Generally, money is viewed by most as a very tangible aspect of any reward system, but other intangible rewards are also effective. Most project team members are motivated by an opportunity to grow, accomplish, and apply their professional skills to meet new challenges. Public recognition of good performance creates positive reinforcement. A good strategy for project managers is to give the team all possible recognition during the life cycle of the project rather than after the project is completed.

204. Answer: A.

PMBOK® Guide Appendix G, Section G.4; and page 243, Introduction

Communication

To communicate effectively, the project manager should be aware of the communication styles of other parties, cultural issues, relationships, personalities, and overall context of the situation. Awareness of these factors leads to mutual understanding and thus to effective communication. Project managers should identify various communication channels, understand what information they need to provide, what information they need to receive, and which interpersonal skills will help them communicate effectively with various project stakeholders. . .

Project Communications Management

Project Communications Management includes the processes required to ensure timely and appropriate generation, collection, distribution, storage, retrieval, and ultimate disposition of project information. Project managers spend the majority of their time communicating with team members and other project stakeholders, whether they are internal (at all organizational levels) or external to the organization. Effective communication creates a bridge between diverse stakeholders involved in a project, connecting various cultural and organizational backgrounds, different levels of expertise, and various perspectives and interests in the project execution or outcome.

205. Answer: C.
PMBOK® Guide Appendix G.7; and page 27, Section 2.4.1

Political and Cultural Awareness
. . . Cultural differences can be both individual and
corporate in nature and may involve both internal and
external stakeholders. An effective way to manage this
cultural diversity is through getting to know the various
team members and the use of good communication
planning as part of the overall project plan.

Culture at a behavioral level includes those behaviors
and expectations that occur independently of
geography, ethnic heritage, or common and disparate
languages. Culture can impact the speed of working,
the decision-making process, and the impulse to act
without appropriate planning. This may lead to conflict
and stress in some organizations, thereby affecting the
performance of project managers and project teams.

Organizational Cultures and Styles
Cultures and styles may have a strong influence on a
project's ability to meet its objectives. Cultures and
styles are typically known as "cultural norms." The
"norms" include a common knowledge regarding how
to approach getting the work done, what means are
considered acceptable for getting the work done, and
who is influential in facilitating the work getting done.

Most organizations have developed unique cultures
that manifest in numerous ways. . .

Kid Pix Digital Gallery

Cameras, Scanners, and Computers

Judy K. Ballweg

Published by International Society for Technology in Education, 2000

Director of Publishing
Jean Marie Hall

Project Coordinator
Corinne Tan

Editor
Christy McMannis, The Electronic Page

Production
Corinne Tan

Cover Design
Signe Landin

© Judy K. Ballweg, 2000
Published by International Society for Technology in Education

Administrative Office
1787 Agate Street
Eugene, OR 97403-1923
Phone: 541.346.4414
Fax: 541.346.5890
E-Mail: iste@oregon.uoregon.edu

Customer Service Office
480 Charnelton Street
Eugene, OR 97401-2626
Order Desk: 800.336.5191
Order Fax: 541.302.3778
E-Mail: cust_svc@iste.org

World Wide Web: www.iste.org

ISBN 1-56484-156-1

From the Publisher

The International Society for Technology in Education (ISTE) promotes appropriate uses of technology to support and improve learning, teaching, and administration. As part of that mission, ISTE's goal is to provide individuals and organizations with high-quality and timely information, materials, and services that support technology in education.

Our Books and Courseware Department works with educators to develop and produce classroom-tested materials and resources that support ISTE's mission. We look for content that emphasizes the use of technology where it can make a difference—making the teacher's job easier; saving time; motivating students; helping students with various learning styles, abilities, or backgrounds; and creating learning environments that are new and unique or that would be impossible without technology.

We develop products for students, classroom teachers, lab teachers, technology coordinators, and teacher educators, as well as for parents, administrators, policy makers, and visionaries. All of us face the challenge of keeping up with new technologies and the research about their educational applications while we are learning about and implementing appropriate applications in our teaching/learning situations. Please help us in our efforts to help you by providing feedback about this book and other ISTE products and by giving us your suggestions for further development.

Jean Marie Hall, Director of Publishing
Phone: 541.346.2519; E-Mail: jhall@iste.org

Anita Best, Acquisitions Editor
Phone: 541.346.2400; E-Mail: abest@iste.org

International Society for Technology in Education
Books and Courseware Department
1787 Agate Street
Eugene, OR 97403-1923

About the Author

Judy K. Ballweg has been a K–2 technology teacher in the Madison Metropolitan School District in Madison, Wisconsin, for five years. During this time she has developed a unique literature-based technology program for her primary students. This book is a collection of activities that Judy has used to introduce the use of digital images and photography. Along with teaching children, Judy has also taught a variety of staff development workshops for staff members in her district.

In her free time, Judy enjoys reading ... especially children's picture books. She also loves walking, watching Wisconsin Badger Basketball, working in her flower beds, graphic design, and writing. She is the author of another ISTE publication, *Kid Pix ABC–Art, Books, and Computers*.

The author welcomes questions or comments about the activities in this book. Please contact her through ISTE.

Dedication

To Jay,
who has never had much luck with photography

Table of Contents

Introduction

Computer Literacy Counts

Our students are growing up at a complicated, challenging, and exciting time. Technology is all around them, and it is rapidly changing and infiltrating every area of society. It has been estimated that "by the year 2010 virtually every job in America will require some use of technology." (Alden, 1998). It is not only language arts and math skills that children need.... All students must also learn to use technology if they wish to live, work, and learn in our world. With support from parents, employers, communities, and the nation, educators must provide meaningful opportunities for students to use and explore available technology in their classrooms. "Technology can enable students to become

❖ capable information technology users

❖ information seekers, analyzers, and evaluators

❖ problem solvers and decision makers

❖ creative and effective users of productivity tools

❖ communicators, collaborators, publishers, and producers

❖ informed, responsible, and contributing citizens" (ISTE, 1998)

Technology also provides many benefits for students in the classroom. Studies show that technology use can help to

❖ bolster children's self-esteem and self-confidence

❖ increase literacy rates

❖ promote visual thinking skills

❖ increase creativity

❖ decrease the number of high school dropouts

❖ increase levels of achievement

❖ individualize instruction

❖ increase attendance, motivation, and attention span

❖ communicate with others around the world

❖ add a new, third dimension to data

❖ increase access to information

❖ practice facts, experiment, and tutor children

❖ provide entertainment

❖ increase productivity

❖ work collaboratively with peers

❖ provoke discussion

❖ expand risk taking

"It is clear that students who become computer literate today will be better prepared to take on future academic and professional challenges with the aid of computers and software." (Alden, 1998) The time has come for our nation to take educational technology seriously.... Computer literacy counts.

How to Use This Book

The activities in this book provide ways to develop vital technology, language arts, and visual arts skills in young students. Each lesson is based on a piece of children's literature and focuses on the use of digital images. Most activities can be completed with the use of a digital camera or scanner. Simple directions for using cameras and scanners are included in this Introduction. The lessons provide detailed directions for reading the stories and demonstrating the coordinating projects on the computer in a whole-group setting. They include learning objectives in primary language arts and technology, based on the national standards provided in the Appendix. The lessons also provide ideas for extension. The instructions are written for use on a Macintosh computer, but most of the instructions will easily transfer for use on a PC with the Windows operating system.

The activities in *Kid Pix Digital Gallery* are divided into sections based on the manner in which the digital image will be used: Meet the Digital Camera and Scanner, Cropping and Importing a Photo, Modifying Photos, and Creating A Gallery. This is the sequence that I have found to work best. Feel free to present the lessons in a sequence that works best for you and the students in your classroom. At the back of the book, you will find some additional applications for digital images, a list of the books mentioned in the activities, and a list of references.

The computer activities in this book have been written for use with Kid Pix Studio Deluxe software by Brøderbund. A description of Kid Pix and basic instructions for using the program are included later in this Introduction. Most activities, however, could be adapted to any graphics program. The lessons provided can be accomplished with one, two, or a lab full of computers. See Miss Judy's Answers for ways to effectively manage the projects in this book. A disk of templates has also been provided so you can focus your energy on the students, not on lesson preparation. A disk icon will appear on the first page of the lesson if a template is supplied for the activity.

You will need a copy of Kid Pix Studio Deluxe to open the templates on the disk. Please note that Internet access will also be necessary for the "Visiting the Art Museum—Online!" lesson.

Miss Judy's Answers to Frequently Asked Questions

How Does a Digital Camera Aid Instruction?

A digital camera works similarly to a standard camera. It can take pictures inside or outside, and the pictures can be used to personalize students' work in the classroom. One difference, however, is that the digital camera does not need film. All of the pictures you take are stored on a disk inside the camera. The pictures are retrieved when you connect the camera to the computer and download them.

A digital camera allows you to

- ❖ see the pictures you take immediately

- ❖ save the pictures you take and use them again and again

- ❖ import the pictures you take into another document or program

- ❖ modify the pictures you take

- ❖ enlarge or reduce the size of the pictures you take

- ❖ print directly from the camera's software

- ❖ save money (because you will not need to pay for film and developing)

- ❖ personalize your students' work

Although there are many types of digital cameras, most have similar features. Some popular digital cameras on the market today are the Sony Mavica, Olympus D-620-L, Epson PhotoPC, Kodak Digital Science, Nikon Coolpix, Connectix QuickCam, and the Apple QuickTake. Simple directions for using a Connectix QuickCam and Apple QuickTake 150 and 200 cameras are included in this Introduction. For specific directions about the camera, consult the owner's manual.

What Is a Scanner?

A scanner works similarly to a photocopier. It can make a digital copy of a photo or illustration. The pictures you scan appear on the computer screen and can be saved and used in the same way as a photo from a digital camera. Thus, scanned images can be used in place of photos from a digital camera in any of the activities in this book. A color scanner allows you to

❖ make a color copy of a photograph or illustration

❖ see the pictures you scan immediately

❖ save the pictures you scan and use them again and again

❖ import the pictures you scan into another document or program

❖ modify the pictures you scan

❖ enlarge or reduce the size of the pictures you scan

❖ print directly from the scanner's software

❖ save money (because you will not need to pay for photo duplication)

❖ personalize your students' work

Although there are many types of scanners, most have similar features. Simple directions for using a Hewlett Packard ScanJet are included in this Introduction. For specific directions about the scanner, consult the owner's manual.

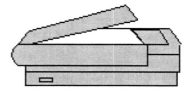

How Can I Effectively Use a Digital Camera or Scanner in My Classroom?

The digital camera and scanner are amazing, practical tools to use in the classroom. They provide opportunities for your students to learn wonderful technological skills, as well as personalize their projects. However, it may be impractical to use a digital camera and scanner in a whole-class situation. Downloading, cropping, and importing pictures can be time-consuming; and your students may get impatient while waiting. How can you effectively use a digital camera and scanner in your classroom?

❖ Use the lessons in this book and the templates provided. These activities provide meaningful ways to teach technology skills through literature. Lessons feature detailed directions, suggestions to make the activities flow more smoothly, and curriculum extensions. A disk of templates has been provided so you can focus your energy on the students, not on lesson preparation.

❖ Always demonstrate each step in the activity to your students. Post a list of required steps and a sample of completed work by the computer. Also display a copy of the book or text that the students may need to copy onto the screen.

❖ Modify the number of steps performed by your students based on their skills and needs. For example, when using an activity in a whole-class, primary-level situation, you would not expect your students to take, download, crop, import, and modify their own photos. Instead you may choose to allow all of your students to take pictures with the digital camera, but plan to download, crop, and import the pictures into Kid Pix yourself after class. The students can then begin working with their pictures right from a Kid Pix document during the next session. Similarly, if a project seems too easy for an intermediate student, make the requirements more difficult. Or, have the student make the project for or with a primary "buddy."

❖ Work with a small group of three to four students at the primary level. Primary students can perform the steps for using the digital camera and scanner, but will require more individual instruction.

❖ Allow intermediate-level students to work with the equipment alone or in pairs (after they have learned the basic skills needed). Provide simple instructions so they can work independently.

❖ Save photos of all of the students on a disk so you can use them again throughout the year. When a lesson in this book asks you to "take a picture of each student," you can simply use a picture saved from a previous activity.

❖ Put a copy of the students' photos on their floppy disks. They can import the photos into other work on the computer. Or, if using a Mac, save the photos to the scrapbook. They can just drag-and-drop them into each document.

❖ Lock all Kid Pix documents that are created for student use. (See the instructions on how to lock a Kid Pix document.) Locking a document prohibits users from saving over the original work. Thus, students cannot accidentally lose the photos that have been cropped and imported into Kid Pix.

❖ Familiarize yourself with the camera and scanner before you attempt to teach them to your students.

What Is Kid Pix?

Kid Pix Studio Deluxe is a graphics program created by Brøderbund for use with elementary students. The activities in this book use the drawing component of the program. Kid Pix features the same drawing tools as other drawing and painting programs, with a few extras. It comes with sets of rubber stamps, which students can use instead of trying to draw all objects freehand. It also has Talking Alphabet Stamps, Electric Mixer, and Moving Van tools. It has an exciting sound library, clip art, maps, pictures to color with the Paint Can tool, and some text-to-speech functions. Kid Pix Studio Deluxe also features Wacky TV, Digital Puppets, Stampimator, Moopies, and SlideShow.

Kid Pix is motivating for elementary students. It is fun, exciting, and easy for children to manipulate. It also provides an infinite number of curriculum connections.

It is important for you, the instructor, to be familiar with the Kid Pix tools before attempting to introduce them to the students. Take time to explore each tool. Try each activity and make a sample before you demonstrate the activity to the students. It is helpful, but not necessary, for the students to have experience with Kid Pix before doing these lessons. *Kid Pix ABC–Art, Books, and Computers*, also by Judy Ballweg, provides lessons designed to teach the Kid Pix tools.

It is important to use the correct names for the tools. This will not only help the students communicate with others more easily and appropriately but it will also help make their transition to another graphics program smoother.

The following Kid Pix tool bar includes a brief description of each tool's basic function. The tool bar runs down the left side of the screen. When you click on a tool, the options for that tool appear at the bottom of the screen.

To learn more about Kid Pix Studio Deluxe, refer to the owner's manual. The Kid Pix manual is very helpful and well organized.

	Wacky Pencil–Draw in a variety of colors, styles, and sizes.
	Line–Draw straight lines in a variety of colors, styles, and sizes.
	Rectangle–Draw boxes in a variety of colors, patterns, and sizes.
	Oval–Draw ovals in a variety of colors, patterns, and sizes.
	Wacky Brush–Paint with a variety of options to create special effects.
	Paint Can–Fill an enclosed space with a color or a pattern.
	Electric Mixer–Mix up the picture in new wacky ways.
	Eraser–Erase part or all of a picture.
	Talking Alphabet Stamps–Stamp letters onto a picture.
	Typewriter–Use the keyboard to enter text to the screen.
	Rubber Stamps–Choose one of 2,912 stamps to add to a picture.
	Moving Van–Highlight graphics or text to be moved, copied, or cut.
	Eyedropper–Match an exact color found in a picture.
	Undo Guy–Undo the last step.

The Color Palette appears at the bottom of the tool bar. Select a color to use with the Wacky Pencil, Line, Rectangle, Oval, Wacky Brush, Paint Can, Talking Alphabet Stamps, or Typewriter tools. Select more colors with the arrows at the bottom of the palette.

How Can I Save Time, Money, and Ink?

1. **Use the available printing options.**

    ❖ Save ink by printing in Medium or Teensy occasionally. Students love minibooks and tiny pictures. (If you click the Manual button when you print, you can also select the percentage at which you wish to print.)

    ❖ When you print, select the Manual button and check the Grayscale box. This will save the colored ink for extra-special projects. Your students can select special colored, preprinted computer paper or embellish their work at an art center. (Work printed in grayscale also seems to photocopy much clearer than work in color, allowing you to make multiple copies.)

    ❖ Insist that your students get your approval and help when printing. This will save ink and paper lost to mistakes.

    ❖ Make it a rule that students may print out one paper during their turns at the computer. This requires students to select their best work.

2. **Find creative alternatives to printing every piece of student work.** "Publishing" doesn't mean that work has to be printed on paper.

    ❖ Combine student work into a SlideShow. Videotape the SlideShow through Televeyes Pro or another presentation system. Then allow students to check out the videotape from the classroom library so they can share their work at home.

    ❖ Provide a floppy disk for students to save finished and unfinished work. Students can open the disk to show work on Open House night or at a parent-teacher conference instead of printing. The family can have the option of purchasing the disk at the end of the school year.

❖ Share your students' work on disk at a group time, or, if you work in a lab situation, have students walk around the computer lab and admire other's work before erasing.

3. **Modify photos in Kid Pix.**

❖ Rather than using the lasso to crop a picture, bring the photo into Kid Pix and erase around it. Start with a small Eraser tool option or thin white pencil. This will allow you to be more precise. Erase a small portion at a time and then release the mouse button. (If you make a mistake and use the Undo Guy, the computer will not undo everything you've erased, only the most recent part.) After you've erased around the subject, you can select a bigger Eraser tool or white pencil to erase the outside portion of the picture.

❖ Move the photos on the screen by using the Moving Van tool.

4. **Lock your documents.**

It is important to lock documents that you have created for student use. A locked document prohibits users from saving over the original work. Students using a locked document will be required to rename the document before they can save a copy. The original template will remain untouched.

You should also lock documents that contain student photos. Locking these documents will protect them from being accidentally erased, marred, or trashed, saving you and the students from having to re-create your work.

To lock a Kid Pix document:

1. Open a Kid Pix document.

2. Create a page, leaving spaces where the students are to add text or graphics.

3. Save your work on a disk. (Select **Save As** from the **File** menu.)

4. Select **Quit** from the **File** menu.

5. Open the disk on the desktop.

6. Click ONCE on the document you just created to highlight it.

7. Select **Get Info** from the **File** menu.

8. When a dialog box appears with the name of the document, check the Locked checkbox in the bottom left corner. Close.

When you open the document, a dialog box will appear stating that the document is locked. You may work on this document as you normally would; however, when you're ready to save, you must select **Save As** and type a name for this new copy.

You can unlock documents by selecting **Get Info** from the **File** menu and unchecking the Locked checkbox. You will need to unlock the documents before you put them in the trash or hold down the Option key when you select **Empty Trash** from the **Special** menu. This will allow the locked documents to be deleted.

Basic Instructions for Using the Apple QuickTake 150 Digital Camera

To Take Pictures

1. Attach the battery pack or AC adapter to the camera.

2. Turn the camera on by opening the front lens cover.

3. For the best quality, set the camera to 16 pictures.

4. Take a picture of the subject by pushing the button on the top of the camera.

To Download Pictures to the Computer

1. Attach one end of the camera cord to the computer modem port and the other end to the camera.

2. Turn the camera on by opening the front lens cover.

3. Open the hard drive, and find the "Photoflash for QuickTake" folder.

4. Open the "Photoflash for QuickTake" folder, and find the Photoflash application.

5. Open Photoflash. Note the change in the menu bar at the top.

6. From the **Script** menu, drag down and over the **QuickTake Scripts** submenu to select **Get All Images**. The pictures will begin to appear, layered, on the screen.

7. You can crop them now, or close them by clicking in the close box in the top left corner of each picture.

To Store Pictures

Pictures will automatically be saved in the "Camera Pictures" folder.

It is important to sort through your pictures and crop them because they use up a lot of computer memory. Move pictures you no longer need into the computer's trash bin.

To Crop a Picture and Save

1. Select a picture to crop and open it.

2. The Photoflash tools are to the left of the photo. The crop tool is already selected for you. Move the pointer to the photo, hold down the mouse button, and draw a box around the subject in the photo.

3. Select **Crop** from the **Image** menu. This will remove the part of the photo outside of the crop box. You can change the size of the photo by selecting **Resize** from the **Image** menu.

4. Save the photo. Select **Save As** from the **File** menu. When the Save As dialog box opens, name the picture and select Pict. CHECK THE LOCATION WHERE THE PHOTO WILL BE SAVED. Then click the Save button.

To Copy and Paste a Picture into Kid Pix (or Another Document)

1. Select the cropped picture and open it.

2. Choose **Select All** from the **Edit** menu. The photo should have a flashing box around it.

3. Select **Copy** from the **Edit** menu.

4. Open the Kid Pix document.

5. Select **Paste** from the **Edit** menu.

6. Move or resize the photo, if necessary.

7. Select **Save A Picture** from the **File** menu to save your work.

To Import a Photo into Kid Pix

1. Open a document.

2. Select **Import a Graphic** from the **File** menu.

3. When the Import a Graphic dialog box opens, locate the image and open it. The image should appear in the document.

4. Move or resize the picture, if necessary.

5. Select **Save A Picture** from the **File** menu to save your work.

To Insert a Photo into an AppleWorks Word-Processing Document

1. Open a word-processing document.

2. Click the pointer in the top left corner of the tool bar. This will insert the picture as a graphic and allow you to move and modify it.

3. Select **Insert** from the **File** menu.

4. When the dialog box opens, locate the image and open it. The image should appear in the word-processing document.

5. Move or resize the photo, if necessary.

6. Select **Save As** from the **File** menu to save your work.

Basic Instructions for Using the Apple QuickTake 200 Digital Camera

The Apple QuickTake 200 camera has the same basic functions as the 150. However, it is much more sophisticated. This camera allows the user to view the subject on an LCD screen or with a viewfinder, zoom in and out, adjust the lighting, set a self-timer, record the date and time, store more images, view the images saved in the camera, download images, upload images, protect images from being erased, view a series of images on a color TV screen, and create QuickTime movies. Steps for completing all of these special functions are explained in detail in the owner's manual. This book provides simple directions for taking and using photos with the QuickTake 200.

To Take Pictures

1. Load the batteries into the bottom of the camera or attach the AC adapter.

2. Turn the camera on, using the sliding power switch above the LCD screen.

3. Erase all pictures stored in the camera. Turn the mode dial to the Garbage Can icon. Note the list of choices on the LCD screen. Use the +/- buttons to move the arrow on the screen to "all." Push the action button next to the +/- buttons two times to erase the storage card. Note: All pictures will remain stored in the camera until you erase them.

4. Turn the mode dial to Record (the checkerboard icon). View the subject through the LCD panel. Adjust the focus and lighting using the switches on the top of the camera.

5. Frame the subject and press the shutter release on the top of the camera to capture the image.

To Download Pictures to the Computer

1. Turn off the camera. Attach the AC adapter to the camera.

2. Hook the serial cable from the camera to the computer modem port.

3. Turn the mode dial to the Computer Mode (the two arrows icon).

4. Turn the camera on by sliding the power switch above the LCD screen. "PC mode" appears on the LCD screen.

5. Open the "QuickTake 200" folder on the hard drive. Double-click the Camera Access icon. Click the Viewer button. The camera's contents will be displayed on the screen. To download all images, select **Copy All Images to Disk** from the **Viewer** menu.

6. In the dialog box that appears, select where you would like the images to be stored. Click the Save button. Open the file and rename each image, if desired.

To Store Pictures

It is important to sort through your pictures and crop them because they use up a lot of computer memory. Move pictures you no longer need into the computer's trash bin.

To Crop a Picture and Save

1. Select a picture to crop and open it.

2. The pointer automatically becomes a cropping tool. Draw a box around the portion of the image to be kept. Select **Crop** from the **Image** menu.

3. Select **Save As** from the **File** menu. Select a name and location for the image. Click the Save button.

To Copy and Paste a Picture into Kid Pix (or Another Document)

1. Select the cropped picture and open it.

2. Choose **Select All** from the **Edit** menu. The photo should have a flashing box around it.

3. Select **Copy** from the **Edit** menu.

4. Open the Kid Pix document.

5. Select **Paste** from the **Edit** menu.

6. Move or resize the photo, if necessary.

7. Select **Save A Picture** from the **File** menu to save your work.

To Import a Photo into Kid Pix

1. Open a document.

2. Select **Import a Graphic** from the **File** menu.

3. When the Import a Graphic dialog box opens, locate the image and open it. The image should appear in the document.

4. Move or resize the picture, if necessary.

5. Select **Save A Picture** from the **File** menu to save your work.

Basic Instructions for Using the Connectix Color QuickCam

The QuickCam provides a way to add live color video to the computer. It can be used to digitize photos and create graphics to be used in Kid Pix and other documents. The QuickCam also has a self-timer and Auto-capture capabilities.

Getting Started

1. TURN OFF THE COMPUTER. (It may damage the computer's logic board to change connections to the ADB port while the computer is on.)

2. Unplug the keyboard. Plug the QuickCam's "T" cable into the ADB port (where the keyboard was plugged in). Plug the keyboard into the "T" cable.

3. Plug the other cable into the modem serial port on the back of the computer. (The modem serial port is the jack with the telephone icon under it.)

4. Put the QuickCam on its base.

5. Turn the computer on.

6. Adjust the lighting in the room so that you can take a picture clearly without the use of a flash.

To Take and Save a Still Picture

1. Open the "QuickCam" folder on the hard drive.

2. Double-click the QuickPICT application. Immediately you will see the image that the QuickCam is focused on.

3. Click the square in the bottom left corner until a disk icon is displayed. (This will allow you to save the image to the disk, rather than to the clipboard on the hard drive.)

4. Adjust the QuickCam so that the subject of the picture is displayed on the computer screen. Focus the QuickCam by turning the focusing ring on the outside of the lens. Select an area of the picture to capture by drawing a box around the image with the mouse. (This will crop the picture and take away the excess background.)

5. Click the Take Picture button with the mouse.

6. At the prompt, type a name for the picture. Click the Desktop button and open the disk. Click the Save button to save the image to the disk.

To Bring a QuickCam Image into Kid Pix

1. Open a document.

2. Select **Import A Graphic** from the **File** menu.

3. When the dialog box opens, locate the image on the disk and open it. The image should appear in the document.

4. Move or resize the picture, if necessary.

5. Select **Save A Picture** from the **File** menu to save your work.

To Bring a QuickCam Image into an AppleWorks Word-Processing Document

1. Open a word-processing document.

2. Click the pointer in the top left corner of the tool bar.

3. Select **Insert** from the **File** menu.

4. When the dialog box opens, locate the image on the disk and open it. The image should appear in the word-processing document.

5. Move or resize the photo, if necessary.

6. Select **Save As** from the **File** menu to save your work.

To Record and Save Images as a Video

1. Open the "QuickCam" folder on the hard drive.

2. Double-click the QuickMovie application. When the dialog box opens, type in a name for the new movie and choose a location in which to save it. Click the New button.

3. Drag the bottom right corner of the screen to adjust the movie size. Note: Larger frames will record fewer frames per second, producing a less fluid-looking video.

4. Adjust the QuickCam so that the subject of the picture is displayed on the computer screen. Focus the QuickCam by turning the focusing ring on the outside of the lens.

5. Click the Record button to record the video. Click the Stop button to pause or stop recording.

6. Save the video by selecting **Save** from the **File** menu.

7. Select **Close** from the **File** menu to close the video.

To View and Edit a QuickCam Video

1. Open the "QuickCam" folder on the hard drive.

2. Select **Open** from the **File** menu.

3. When the dialog box opens, locate the video and click the Open button.

4. View the video by clicking the small arrow (on the left, below the saved image).

5. To insert a new video clip, place the thumb on the slider at the point where the new video will be added. Click the QuickCam icon in the bottom left corner to switch to record mode. Click the Record button to record the new video. Click the Stop button to pause or stop recording. View the video by clicking the small arrow.

Basic Instructions for Using the Hewlett Packard ScanJet Scanner

To Prescan an Image

1. Make sure the scanner is correctly connected to the computer.

2. Turn on the scanner.

3. Turn on the computer.

4. Open the hard drive and find the DeskScan II application.

5. Open the DeskScan II application.

6. Place the picture face-down in the top corner of the scanner.

7. Choose the appropriate type of picture from the Type pull-down menu.

8. Click the Preview button to make a prescan.

9. Click the Zoom button, if you wish, to bring the image closer.

To Adjust the Image

1. Resize the flashing box around the image to select the portion of the picture to be kept. Grab the corners of the box and drag with the mouse to crop. Note: This will change the scale of the image (the width and height) as well as the size of the file.

2. Proportionally change the scale of the picture by clicking the arrows at the left or right ends of the scaling slide bar. This will also change the size of the file. (If you plan to put the image on a floppy disk, the file cannot exceed 1,400 K.)

3. Adjust the brightness, contrast, image reverse, or negative, if you wish.

To Do a Final Scan and Save

1. Click the Final button at the bottom of the screen. A dialog box will appear to select where the image should be saved.

2. Click the Desktop button. (Because of memory issues, save to the desktop first.)

3. Type a name for the image. Click the Save button. The scanner will scan the image to the file you have named. You will see the file on the desktop. (The icon is a picture of a scanner.)

4. Drag the file onto a disk. A dialog box should appear that reads "Copy. Items remaining to be copied: 1."

5. Open the floppy disk and verify that the file is there.

6. Drag the file from the desktop to the trash. Select **Empty Trash** from the **Special** menu. Click the OK button.

7. Remove the picture from the scanner.

To Bring a Scanned Image into Kid Pix

1. Open a document.

2. Select **Import a Graphic** from the **File** menu.

3. When the dialog box opens, locate the image on the disk and open it. The image should appear in the document.

4. Modify the picture, if necessary.

5. Select **Save A Picture** from the **File** menu to save your work.

To Bring a Scanned Image into an AppleWorks Word-Processing Document

1. Open a word-processing document.

2. Click the pointer in the top left corner of the tool bar.

3. Select **Insert** from the **File** menu.

4. When the dialog box opens, locate the image on the disk and open it. The image should appear in the word-processing document.

5. Move or resize the picture, if necessary.

6. Select **Save As** from the **File** menu to save your work.

Student Activities

Meet the Digital Camera and Scanner

Click! A Book about
Cameras and Taking Pictures

based on the book by Gail Gibbons

Technical Objectives

❖ introduce the basic care and use of a digital camera

❖ compare care and use of a digital camera to that of a standard camera

❖ use technology resources for directed and independent learning activities

❖ work collaboratively with others when using technology in the classroom

Language Arts Objectives

❖ read nonfiction materials to gain information about a topic

❖ use words to describe and compare objects and actions

❖ participate in a discussion about what is being learned

❖ extend vocabulary

Introductory Activities

❖ Read *Click! A Book about Cameras and Taking Pictures* by Gail Gibbons to the students.

❖ Point out the basic parts on a standard camera as you read the book: flash, shutter, lens, view finder, frame counter, film advance lever, aperture, back door release button. Demonstrate how to load and advance the film.

❖ Explain how to properly care for a camera. (Hold it carefully. Use the strap. Do not let the camera fall. Clean the lens with a soft cloth. Keep the camera dry. Do not open the camera until the film is used up and rewound. Store the camera and film in its case in a cool, dry place.)

❖ Allow your students to take pictures using a variety of cameras: compact, single-lens reflex, single-use, disc, pocket, underwater, and instamatic.

❖ Visit a photo processing lab or a professional photographer's studio to see how film is developed.

❖ Combine the class photos into a class photo album. Students can word process a caption to add with their pictures. Do not glue the pictures down, as the students will use these pictures when they begin scanning. (Keep those negatives handy, too. You can use them for the "Time Capsule!" lesson.)

Computer Activity

❖ Introduce the digital camera. Demonstrate how to properly care for a digital camera. (Hold it carefully. Use the strap. Do not let the camera fall. Clean the lens with a soft cloth. Keep the camera dry. Store the camera in its case in a cool, dry place.)

❖ Point out the basic parts on the digital camera: flash, shutter, lens, view finder, frame counter. Demonstrate how to select the number of pictures available and erase the pictures when the camera is full.

❖ Have students take pictures of each other using the digital camera. Download the students' pictures so that they can see them on the computer. Crop and save the pictures for use in other projects. Print a picture for each student.

❖ Open the "Camera Venn Diagram" template on the disk provided. As a class, list ways that a digital camera and standard camera are the same and different.

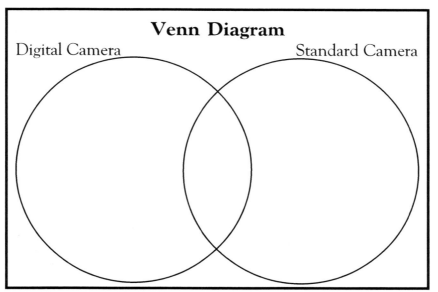

Extensions

❖ Make pin-hole cameras. See the books *Cameras* by Chris Oxlade and *My First Photography Book* by Dave King for instructions on how to do this. These books have science experiments for recording, printing, and projecting images; making a zoetrope; using lenses, light, and filters; focal lengths; and animation. King's book also demonstrates how to use film, take pictures, crop, matte, enlarge, add special effects, and make a photographer's kit. Make King's mini-play theater with digital photos and scenery made on the computer.

❖ Share other great picture books about cameras: *Pascual's Magic Pictures* by Amy Glaser Gage, *Pig Pig and the Magic Photo Album* by David McPhail, *Grandpa Baxter and the Photographs* by Caroline Castle and Peter Bowman, *Simple Pictures Are Best* by Nancy Willard, *One Bear in the Picture* by Caroline Bucknall, *My Camera* by Harriet Ziefert, and *My Camera at the Aquarium* by Janet Perry Marshall.

My First ABC

based on the book by Jane Bunting

Technical Objectives

❖ take close-up pictures of objects

❖ crop and resize digital images

❖ use input and output devices to successfully operate computers and other technologies

❖ use technology resources for directed and independent learning activities

❖ use developmentally appropriate multimedia resources to support learning

❖ work collaboratively with others when using technology in the classroom

❖ create developmentally appropriate multimedia products

Language Arts Objectives

❖ identify upper- and lowercase letters

❖ identify beginning sounds

❖ use words to name common objects

❖ generate ideas

❖ write a list

❖ follow directions

❖ use picture cues when reading

❖ publish written and illustrated work

Introductory Activities

❖ Share *My First ABC* by Jane Bunting with the students. Talk about how the illustrations in the book were created (photography). Brainstorm a list of additional objects that begin with each letter. Which objects could be found at school?

❖ Demonstrate how to take pictures using a digital camera. Use the zoom function, if available, to take close-up pictures of small objects.

❖ Demonstrate how to download, crop, resize, and import pictures into Kid Pix, using the resources in this book and the owner's manuals.

❖ Assign a letter of the alphabet to each student.

Computer Activity

❖ During their turns with the camera, students should take pictures of objects that begin with their designated letters.

❖ Students download, crop, resize, and import their pictures into new documents.

❖ They erase around the pictures using the Eraser tool, if desired.

❖ They use the Typewriter tool to write the alphabet letter represented on the page (upper- and lowercase). They write the name of each object next to each picture.

❖ Print. Combine all of the pages into an alphabet book for your classroom.

Extensions

❖ Create an ABC book using scanned images.

❖ Many other books by Dorling Kindersley Publishing Company use photographs as illustrations. Use the following DK books as patterns (just like *My First ABC*). Create your own classroom reference library.

My Big Book of Everything by Roger Priddy

Counting Book by Dave King

Alphabet Book by Dave King

My First Dictionary by Betty Root

My First Action Word Book by Jane Bunting

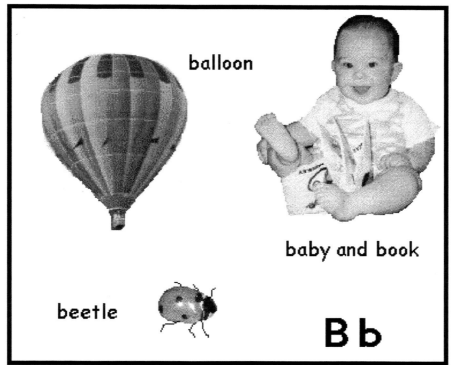

Click!

based on the book by Rhonda Cox

Technical Objectives

❖ frame an image (see the image you want in the view finder)

❖ crop and resize digital images

❖ import a digital image

❖ use technology resources for illustration of thoughts, ideas, and stories

❖ create developmentally appropriate multimedia products

❖ work collaboratively with others when using technology in the classroom

Language Arts Objectives

❖ follow directions with multiple steps

❖ repeat a pattern

❖ publish written and illustrated work

Introductory Activities

❖ Read *Click!* by Rhonda Cox to the students.

❖ Demonstrate how to frame an image using the digital camera.

    1. Take a few steps away from the subject. (For example, you should be about 6 feet away from the subject to get a clear picture with an Apple QuickTake 150 camera.)

    2. Move your body forward, backward, or sideways until the subject is centered in the view finder.

    3. Hold the camera still, so the picture will not be blurry.

    4. Take three pictures of a student in three different poses.

❖ Use the three photos to demonstrate the following computer activity: Making a Minibook of Pictures.

Computer Activity

Use the digital camera directions in this book (or the owner's manual for the camera) to complete the following tasks:

❖ Take three pictures of a partner. Download the images from the camera. Open each picture. Resize and crop each picture until it is about three inches square. Name and save each picture.

❖ Students open the "Click 1" template on the disk provided. They type the author's name on the cover. They type the subject's name, location, and room number on page 1. They decorate the pages, if desired. They save or print "Click 1."

❖ Students open the "Click 2" template on the disk provided. They copy and paste one picture of the subject into the box on page 2. They copy and paste another picture of the subject into the box on page 3. They read the text and delete the "s" on "she" if they're boys. They save or print "Click 2."

❖ Students open the "Click 3" template on the disk provided. They copy and paste the third picture of the subject into the box on page 4. They read the text and erase the "s" on "she" if they're boys. They save or print "Click 3."

❖ They cut the pages in half and combine the pages into a minibook.

Extensions

❖ Use masks, costumes, and face paint to transform the students into animals. Have students pretend they are zoo animals when they pose for the pictures. Change the words in the text to fit each animal.

❖ Share the book *My Camera at the Zoo* by Janet Perry Marshall. Take a trip to a local zoo and photograph the animals.

❖ Read *Faces* by Janie Everett. Take pictures of your students as they display different facial expressions. Use the pictures of your students' faces to create your own book of faces. Use Janie Everett's text, or create the text together.

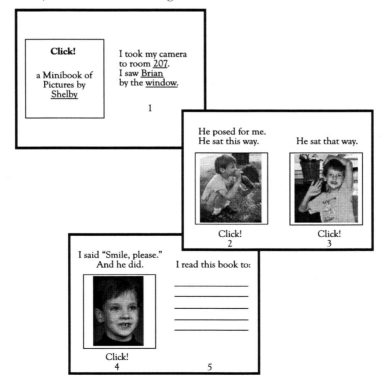

"Reading Rainbow"
Book Talk Video

Technical Objectives

❖ introduce the basic use of a QuickCam and other video equipment

❖ use input and output devices to successfully operate computers and other technologies

❖ work collaboratively with others when using technology in the classroom

❖ practice responsible use of technology

❖ create developmentally appropriate multimedia products

Language Arts Objectives

❖ listen and respond to a variety of media

❖ select appropriate books and topics for writing

❖ use personal experiences, background knowledge, and personal preferences to interpret books

❖ present information in written and oral form

❖ use personal voice in writing

❖ use language to inform, persuade, and entertain

❖ share writing with an audience

Introductory Activities

❖ View Reading Rainbow videos, particularly the short book talks given by students near the end of the tapes.

❖ Brainstorm important ideas that should be included in a book talk: title, author, plot description (without giving away the ending), reasons to read the book, and so on.

❖ Demonstrate the following computer activity: Creating a Book Talk Video.

Computer Activity

❖ Students select a favorite book (or read a new book).

❖ They write a short script that will tell an audience about the book. They can use the sample scripts on the next page as examples. They practice reading their scripts several times until they are memorized.

❖ Students use a QuickCam or other video equipment to record themselves talking about the books. (Directions for recording video clips with a QuickCam are included in the Introduction.)

Extensions

❖ Import the video clip into a Kid Pix document.

❖ Create a Children's Book Review Web page with your class. Import the video clips.

❖ Make a Kid Pix SlideShow about a favorite book. Add pictures you've scanned from the book.

❖ Assign a topic for the whole class. Ask students to select a book about that topic and create a video book talk. Record all of the book talks on videotape (using Apple Televeyes Pro or another presentation system) and share them with another class.

Sample Book Talk Scripts

Hi, I'm Katarina, and I'm a shutterbug! If you like taking pictures, then you'll love *Cameras* by Chris Oxlade. This book shows many different kinds of cameras and how they work. It has really great photographs, too! One thing I enjoyed about this book was the science experiments. This book has experiments to teach how images are projected, recorded, and printed. There are also experiments that use lenses, light, and filters. I liked reading *Cameras* by Chris Oxlade and trying the experiments. I learned a lot, and I know you will, too!

Have you ever gotten pictures back from the photographer and you hate the way you look in them? That's the way Harry feels in this funny book by Kathy Caple, *Harry's Smile*. Harry has a pen pal named Wilma. When Wilma sends Harry a nice photograph of herself, Harry wants to send her a picture of himself. So Harry gets dressed up and goes to the photographer. He tries to look like a movie star, but when he gets his pictures back he hates the way he looks. Harry says he will never smile again! Harry's friends have to try to cheer him up, and that's not easy! This is Zachary saying "Read *Harry's Smile* by Kathy Caple to find out how Harry gets his smile back!"

I just love to wear hats! Hi, I'm Shelby, and I just read this great book called *Hats, Hats, Hats* by Ann Morris. I chose this book because it has interesting photographs by Ken Heyman that were taken all over the world. There are people wearing hats from Japan, Egypt, Peru, England, Indonesia, Nigeria, El Salvador, and the United States. Ann Morris tells about each of the hats at the end of the book. If you like books with photographs and you like to learn about people of other cultures, you'll love *Hats, Hats, Hats* by Ann Morris. Hats off to this great book!

Time Capsule!

Technical Objectives

❖ introduce the basic use of a scanner

❖ import a digital image

❖ demonstrate positive social and ethical behaviors when using technology

❖ create developmentally appropriate multimedia products

Language Arts Objectives

❖ recognize that information is gained from books and nonprint materials

❖ make a list

❖ use words to name objects, people, and actions

❖ write in complete sentences using appropriate punctuation and capital letters

❖ write an autobiographical account

Introductory Activities

❖ Photocopy a few pages about a famous person you've been studying. Put the pages into a canister, along with some objects that could have belonged to that person. Bury the canister on school grounds. Go on a scavenger hunt with your students and dig up the items you buried. Study them.... What can your students learn about this person by viewing the materials in the can?

❖ Talk about ways we can learn about a person or group of people who lived in the past. We read accounts written by and about them. We look at pictures to see what life was like. We study the tools, clothes, games, homes, vehicles, and money they used. Your special class should not be forgotten in history. Make a time capsule to teach others what life is like in your classroom right now.

❖ Brainstorm a list of important things that could be included in the time capsule.

❖ Review the class photo album created in the "Click! A Book about Cameras and Taking Pictures" lesson, and select pictures that will be scanned and placed in the time capsule. Make sure there is a photo of each student. Scan a whole-class picture and pictures of objects, books, money, tickets, clothes, games, and homes that your students mention on their pages. Add these pictures (with captions) to the time capsule. You may also wish to include a letter to future students.

❖ Demonstrate the following activity: Creating a Class Time Capsule.

Computer Activity

❖ Students scan a photograph of themselves. (Directions for using an HP ScanJet are included in the Introduction. See the owner's manual for more specific directions about the scanner.) They resize the image until it is about 2" X 3". They open the "Time Capsule" template on the disk provided and import the photograph.

❖ Students use the Typewriter tool to fill in the blanks in the document. More blanks are available on the bottom of the screen to add ideas that came up during the brainstorming session. They decorate with other Kid Pix tools, if desired, and print.

❖ After students have created their own autobiographical pages (and any other pages that you agree to add to the time capsule), photocopy all of the pages for each student in the class. Buy or make cardboard canisters with lids. Ask students to create labels for their time capsules (in Kid Pix, of course). Roll up a copy of the class' information and put it in each cylinder. Each student can take a completed time capsule home to open in 5–10 years.

❖ Keep a copy of the time capsule for yourself. Pass one on to succeeding teachers to open with these students when they are ready to graduate from high school. Have a ceremony to bury one copy on the school grounds. Create a map on the computer showing where the time capsule is buried so future students can find it and dig it up.

My name is <u>Nicole</u>. I am <u>7</u> years old.

I am in <u>Miss Judy's</u> class at <u>Midvale Elementary School</u>.
At school, I like <u>to use the computer</u>.
My class has been learning about <u>the ocean</u>.

I like to <u>ride my bike, play Barbies, and read</u>.
My favorite game is <u>Monopoly</u>.
My favorite movie is <u>Mulan</u>.
My favorite book is <u>Chicka Chicka Boom Boom</u>.

_____

_____

Extensions

❖ Add pages about current events in the community and the world. Scan pictures and articles from newspapers and magazines to add to the time capsule. Add a photo of the president, current movie listings, and so on.

❖ View the set of negatives that you received when the photographs were returned from the processor. Compare them to the actual photos. What do your students notice about the colors? Use the Negative button displayed on the scanner's software to create a negative of the image you scanned. Print.

❖ Share *Grandmother's Chair* by Ann Herbert Scott. In this beautiful book, a grandmother and granddaughter use old photographs to trace the history of an heirloom across four generations.

Student Activities

Cropping and Importing a Photo

Love You Forever

based on the book by Robert Munsch

Technical Objectives

❖ import a graphic into a document

❖ modify a graphic

❖ use technology resources for illustration of thoughts, ideas, and stories

❖ use input and output devices to successfully operate computers and other technologies

❖ create developmentally appropriate multimedia products

Language Arts Objectives

❖ identify a pattern in a story

❖ retell a story, sequencing the events

❖ extend a story

❖ publish written and illustrated work

Introductory Activities

❖ Read *Love You Forever* by Robert Munsch to the students. Retell the story as a class, capturing each stage of the main character's life.

❖ Take a picture of the students in the class. Crop and resize each photo to 4" X 6".

❖ Demonstrate the following computer activity: Making a Jigsaw Puzzle.

Computer Activity

❖ Students open the "Love You Forever" template on the disk provided. They insert their pictures inside the frame. They decorate around the pictures, if desired, and save. (Do not decorate outside of the frame. This portion will be cut off later.)

❖ Students select the Wacky Pencil tool. They carefully draw lines over their images to create puzzle pieces and print.

❖ They cut around the frame and discard the extra paper. They carefully cut out the puzzle pieces.

❖ Students decorate a page in Kid Pix. They add the words "Love You Forever" and print. They fold the page into an envelope to hold the puzzle pieces. They make a gift tag for a special family member that says "I Love You to Pieces."

Extensions

❖ Use the "Love You Forever" template as a frame for a special photo.

❖ Try the variety of challenging picture puzzles on *Math Workshop* CD by Brøderbund. *Math Workshop* CD offers puzzles with pictures, patterns, lines, and photographs for K–6 students.

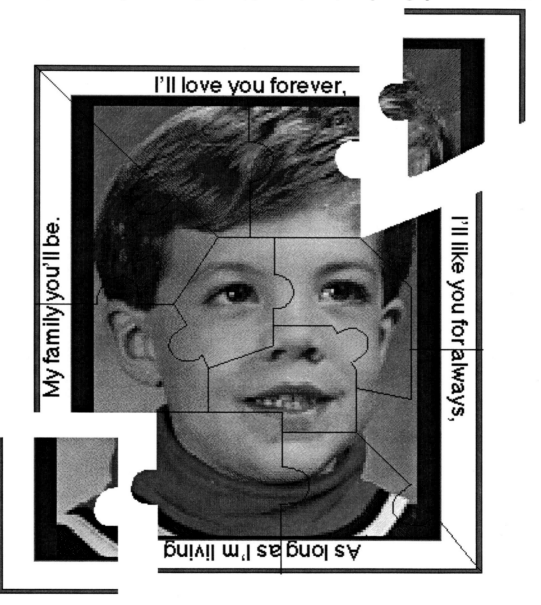

Harry's Smile

based on the book by Kathy Caple

Technical Objectives

❖ import a graphic into a document

❖ modify a graphic

❖ add text to a document

❖ demonstrate positive social and ethical behaviors when using technology

❖ use input and output devices to successfully operate computers and other technologies

❖ create developmentally appropriate multimedia products

Language Arts Objectives

❖ make predictions and give support

❖ explain the problem and solution in a story

❖ write a letter

❖ publish written and illustrated work

Introductory Activities

❖ Read *Harry's Smile* by Kathy Caple to the students. Discuss Harry's problem and some possible solutions.

❖ Take a picture of the students in the class. Crop and resize each photo to about 1" X 2". Save and lock.

❖ Demonstrate the following computer activity: Creating Personalized Stationery.

Computer Activity

❖ Students open a new document. They draw a 3" X 7" rectangle across the screen. They import their photos into the rectangle. They decorate around the photos (within the rectangle) using the Kid Pix tools and save.

❖ Students copy and paste the rectangle with the photo image into the top or bottom corner of a word-processing document. They draw a line with the Line tool to separate the letterhead from the text of the letter. They use the Typewriter tool to add their names, addresses, and slogans next to the photo above the line. They save and lock the documents.

❖ Students open this document every time they want to type a personal letter. Or, they print multiple copies of their letterhead; they can use them to handwrite letters to pen pals.

Extensions

❖ Read *Children Just Like Me: A Unique Celebration of Children around the World* by Barnabas and Anabel Kindersley. Write autobiographies like those in the book. Then, join the Children Just Like Me Pen Pal Club. Send the autobiographies, photos, and letters on the new letterheads to new friends.

To join the club, fill out the application at the end of *Children Just Like Me*, or send name, address, birthdate, gender, parent/guardian signature, and $5.00 check or money order per student to:

> Make A Friend
> Children Just Like Me Pen Pal Club
> DK Publishing, Inc.
> 95 Madison Avenue
> New York, NY 10016

The $5.00 membership fee will be donated to UNICEF, the United Nations Children's Fund.

Along with the above information, the applicant may specify the preferred age of the pen pal (7, 8, 9, 10, 11, 12, 13, 14), the preferred gender of the pen pal (boy, girl), and the home country of the pen pal (Australia, Austria, Brazil, Canada, China, Denmark, France, Germany, India, Italy, Japan, New Zealand, Philippines, South Korea, Spain, Sweden, United Kingdom, West Indies). Also state whether the applicant would prefer to correspond in English or the pen pal's native language. In approximately one month, the club will match students with pen pals that most closely fit their specifications.

❖ Pair up with another class to create e-mail pen pals.

❖ Share *Arthur's Pen Pal* by Lillian Hoban and *Dear Bear* by Joanna Harrison, two more books with pen pals.

Flower Garden

based on the book by Eve Bunting

Technical Objectives

❖ import a graphic into a document

❖ modify a graphic

❖ crop a digital photo

❖ create a 3-D product

❖ create developmentally appropriate multimedia products

❖ use developmentally appropriate multimedia resources to support learning

Language Arts Objectives

❖ listen to contemporary literature

❖ identify rhyming words

❖ identify patterns in text

❖ make predictions and give support

❖ extend vocabulary

❖ publish written and illustrated work

Materials Needed

❖ small round cups (to plant in), one per student

❖ potting soil

❖ flower seeds

Introductory Activities

❖ Read *Flower Garden* by Eve Bunting to the students.

❖ Talk about the tools and flowers shown in the pictures.

❖ Plant flower seeds with the students in small round cups.

❖ Take a picture of the students in the class. Crop and resize the photo to about 1" X 2". Save and lock.

❖ Demonstrate the following computer activity: Creating a Flower Pot Wrapper.

Computer Activity

❖ Students open the "Flower Garden" template on the disk provided. They copy and paste four copies of their photos into the boxes on the screen and save. They decorate the photos in four different ways using the graphics tools. They add text if desired and print.

❖ Students cut out the rectangle with the photos in it and laminate it. They wrap the laminated paper around the flower cup and tape it.

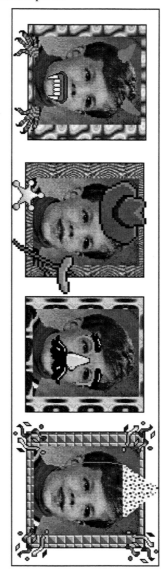

Extensions

❖ Create Mother's Day or birthday cards on the computer, and give the plants as gifts.

❖ Repeat the activity using larger photos and cover juice cans and larger containers. Use these items as pen holders or vases.

Look! Look! Look!

based on the book by Tana Hoban

Technical Objectives

❖ crop a digital picture

❖ import a picture into a document and add text

❖ use input and output devices to successfully operate computers and other technologies

❖ practice responsible use of technology

❖ create developmentally appropriate multimedia products

Language Arts Objectives

❖ use words to describe and name people, places, and things

❖ make predictions and give support

❖ extend a story

❖ publish written and illustrated work

Introductory Activities

❖ Share *Look! Look! Look!* by Tana Hoban with the students. Each page shows part of a picture through a window. Ask students to guess what the whole picture is.

❖ Take a picture of the students in the class. Crop and resize each photo to about 4" X 5". Save and lock. Crop the pictures again, this time selecting only the students' eyes. Select **Save As** from the **File** menu and save this picture under a different name.

❖ Demonstrate the following computer activity, using photos of the students: Make Your Own Class Book—"Look! Look! Look! Who's Eyes Do You Spy?"

Computer Activity

❖ Students open the "Look" template on the disk provided. They copy and paste their pictures into the box on the right half of the screen. They write their names below the photos. They copy and paste the pictures of their eyes into the box on the left half of the screen and print.

❖ Students cut the paper in half. They mount each half on a 4.5" X 6" piece of construction paper (so they can't peek through). Combine all of the students' pictures into a class book, using the "Look! Look! Look! Cover" template provided on the disk. Share the book. Can the students guess whom each pair of eyes belongs to?

Extensions

❖ Add a surprise at the end of the book, like the class guinea pig's eyes.

❖ Crop other parts of the students' faces to create new books: "Look! Look! Look! Whose Nose, Do You Suppose?," "Look! Look! Look! Three Cheers for Ears!," "Look! Look! Look! Whose Chin and Grin?"

❖ Share other books by Tana Hoban with the same format: *Take Another Look, Look Book, Just Look, Look Again.*

❖ Try Nigel's World Geography, a computer program by Lawrence Productions. In this program, students will be asked to follow clues and travel to various continents, countries, and cities to take pictures of a native person, place, and animal. Although Nigel, his home, and office are animated, the photographs used in this program are real. Each photograph is accompanied by factual text about the subject.

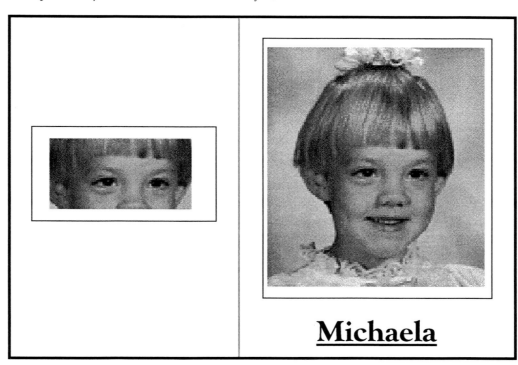

Michaela

Animal Clues

based on the book by David Drew

Technical Objectives

❖ crop a digital picture

❖ import a picture into a document and add text

❖ use input and output devices to successfully operate computers and other technologies

❖ practice responsible use of technology

❖ create developmentally appropriate multimedia products

Language Arts Objectives

❖ use words to describe and name people, places, and things

❖ make predictions and give support

❖ extend a story

❖ publish written and illustrated work

Introductory Activities

❖ Share *Animal Clues* by David Drew with the students. Study the photos and text to guess what the creatures are.

❖ Take a picture of the students in the class. They may then each take two pictures of a feature or a possession. Crop and resize the photos to about 2" X 3". Save and lock each picture.

❖ Demonstrate the following computer activity, using photos of the students: Make Your Own Class Book—"Classroom Clues."

Computer Activity

❖ Students open the "Clues" template on the disk provided. They copy and paste their pictures in the box on the right half of the screen. They write their names below the photos. They copy and paste the two pictures of their features in the boxes on the left half of the screen. They fill in the blanks above and below the pictures: " Here is my _____ and here is my _____. I am ... _____." Print.

❖ Students cut the paper in half. They mount the halves back-to-back on a 4.5" X 6" piece of construction paper.

❖ Combine all of the students' pages into a class book, using the "Classroom Clues Cover" template provided on the disk. This is a book that your students will enjoy reading again and again.

Here are my <u>eyes</u>.

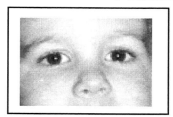

And here are my <u>hands</u>.

I am ...

<u>Ian!</u>

Extensions

❖ Help students scan photos of animals from a book. Crop two features from the animal photos. Copy and paste the pictures into the "Clues" template, and add clues to describe the animals. Create a class book of animal clues.

❖ Use the scanner and the "Clues" template to create a class guessing book, such as "Favorite Picture Book Characters," "Adults in the School," "Toys and Games," and so on.

❖ Share *Mystery Monsters*, another animal guessing book by David Drew.

Look Closer

based on the book by Peter Ziebel

Technical Objectives

- ❖ crop a digital picture
- ❖ import a picture into a document and add text
- ❖ use input and output devices to successfully operate computers and other technologies
- ❖ practice responsible use of technology
- ❖ create developmentally appropriate multimedia products

Language Arts Objectives

- ❖ use words to describe and name people, places, and things
- ❖ make predictions and give support
- ❖ extend a story
- ❖ publish written and illustrated work

Introductory Activities

- ❖ Share *Look Closer* by Peter Ziebel with the students. Study the photos and read the questions. Ask the students to make guesses about the photos before and after you read the questions.
- ❖ Students select objects in the classroom. Take pictures of the students using or next to those objects. Then the students take pictures of the objects by themselves.
- ❖ Download and crop the pictures. Crop the picture of the object so that only part of the object is revealed. Resize both pictures to about 4" X 4". Save and lock each picture.
- ❖ Demonstrate the following computer activity, using photos of common classroom objects: Create Your Own Class Book—"Look Closer."

Computer Activity

- ❖ Students open the "Look Closer!" template on the disk provided. They copy and paste the cropped pictures of the objects in the box on the left half of the screen. Below the photos, they write questions about the objects. They copy and paste their pictures using the objects in the box on the right half of the screen. Below the pictures, they write the names of the objects and print.
- ❖ They cut the paper in half. They mount the halves back-to-back on a 4.5" X 6" piece of construction paper. Combine all of the students' pages into a class book, using the "Look Closer! Cover" template provided on the disk. Share the book with your students.

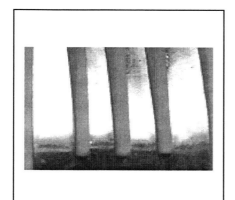

What do you use to eat your birthday cake?

A fork.

Extensions

❖ Share *Mouse Views: What the Class Pet Saw* by Bruce McMillan. Use the camera and the "Look Closer!" template to create a class guessing book, such as "Classroom Jobs," "Adults in the School," "Classroom Pets," "School Supplies," and so on.

❖ Share the book *Come Look with Me: Discovering Photographs with Children* by University of Missouri–St. Louis Art History Professor Jean S. Tucker. This book presents 12 photographs of children taken by American photographers. A short background about each picture and how it was taken accompanies each photo, along with open-ended questions for you and your students. This book is designed to help elementary students understand perspective, color, composition, and the process of photography.

❖ Look at the photographs in the Kid Pix clip art. (Select **Clip Art** from the **Pick More Pictures** submenu in the **Goodies** menu.) History, Presidents, and Yesteryear all have a nice variety of historical photographs. Bring the photos into Kid Pix and write about the subjects. When or how do you think the photos were taken, based on what you know about history and photography (from *Come Look with Me*)?

Alligators and Others All Year Long: A Book of Months

based on the book by Crescent Dragonwagon

Technical Objectives

❖ import a graphic into a document

❖ modify a graphic

❖ use technology resources for directed and independent learning activities

❖ use developmentally appropriate multimedia resources to support learning

❖ work collaboratively with others when using technology in the classroom

❖ create developmentally appropriate multimedia products

Language Arts Objectives

❖ listen to poetry

❖ identify rhyming words

❖ identify high-frequency words

❖ sequence objects, words, and events

❖ publish written and illustrated work

Introductory Activities

❖ Review the names of the months and their order, using a calendar.

❖ Cut the calendar apart. Cut around the set of boxes that make up the days of each month. Glue the 12 sets of boxes together, in order, to show 365 consecutive days. (For example, January 31, Tuesday, should be glued next to February 1, Wednesday.)

❖ Write special holidays and events in the boxes. Include student birthdays, field trips, and important school events. Add small icons to symbolize these special days.

❖ Read *Alligators and Others All Year Long: A Book of Months* by Crescent Dragonwagon to the students.

❖ Take pictures of the students in the class. Crop and resize each photo to 4" X 6".

❖ Demonstrate the following activity: Creating a Personalized Calendar.

Computer Activity

❖ Students open the "Calendar Topper" template on the disk provided. They insert their pictures into the box, save, and lock the documents. They decorate around the photos and print.

❖ They open the "Calendar" template on the disk provided. They use the Typewriter tool to fill in the name of the month at the top of the calendar. They add the numbers to correspond to the days in the boxes.

❖ Students select the Rubber Stamps tool to add rubber stamps that symbolize important events to the appropriate boxes and print. They repeat this process for all 12 months. Note: Younger students could just decorate the current month. They could make and add a new page every four weeks.

❖ Students choose a 12" X 18" piece of heavy tagboard or construction paper. They attach the calendar topper (with their picture) to the top half of the paper. They put the calendar pages in order and staple them together across the top of the sheets. They attach the calendar pages to the bottom half of the 12" X 18" paper.

Extensions

❖ Share *A Year for Kiko* by Ferida Wolff, *A Year with Molly and Emmett* by Marilyn Hafner, and *Calendarbears* by Kathleen Hague; three more great books about months.

❖ Let friends or grandparents know you enjoy "spending time" with them. Read *Grandma's Promise* by Elaine Moore, *The Grandpa Days* by Joan W. Blos, and *My Day with Anka* by Nan Ferring Nelson. Create a calendar for a special adult, grandparent, or friend. Add stamps that show activities you enjoy doing together.

<u>Nicole</u> All Year Long!

 ### October

1	2	3	4	5	6	7
8	9	10	11	12	13	14
15	16	17	18	19	20	21
22	23	24	25	26	27	28
29	30	31				

Student Activities

Modifying Photos

Appelemando's Dreams

based on the book by Patricia Polacco

Technical Objectives

- ❖ import a graphic into a document
- ❖ crop around an image
- ❖ add text to a document
- ❖ use input and output devices to successfully operate computers and other technologies
- ❖ use developmentally appropriate multimedia resources to support learning
- ❖ use technology resources for communication and illustration of thoughts, ideas, and stories
- ❖ create developmentally appropriate multimedia products

Language Arts Objectives

- ❖ make predictions and give support
- ❖ explain the problem and solution in a story
- ❖ retell a story using beginning, middle, and end
- ❖ write in complete sentences, using appropriate punctuation and capital letters
- ❖ publish written and illustrated work

Introductory Activities

- ❖ Scan and import a large photo of each student's head into a document. Remove the background around the head and shoulders with the Eraser tool. Move the image to the bottom left corner of the screen. Save and lock each document.
- ❖ Read *Appelemando's Dreams* by Patricia Polacco to the students and discuss.
- ❖ Demonstrate the following computer activity: I Have a Dream.

Computer Activity

- ❖ Student's open the documents with their cropped heads (from directions above).
- ❖ They select the Wacky Brush tool. At the bottom of the screen, they select the Thought Bubble tool option. They paint a large thought bubble on the right part of the screen.
- ❖ They use other Wacky Brush tool options and the Wacky Pencil tool to draw dreams in the thought bubble. They write about the dreams that were captured.
- ❖ Print. Hang the dreams on a clothesline across the classroom, just like Appelemando's friends did.

Extensions

❖ In celebration of Martin Luther King, Jr.'s Birthday, discuss dreams that famous Americans have had for our country. Scan pictures of these people from books. Write about their dreams and how their dreams helped Americans.

My Head Is Full of Colors

based on the book by Catherine Friend

Technical Objectives

❖ import a graphic into a document

❖ crop around an image

❖ modify a graphic

❖ add text to a document

❖ use technology resources for illustration of thoughts, ideas, and stories

❖ create developmentally appropriate multimedia products

Language Arts Objectives

❖ listen to contemporary literature

❖ make predictions and give support

❖ use words to name objects

❖ extend a story

❖ publish written and illustrated work

Introductory Activities

❖ Scan and import a large photo of each student's head into a document. Remove the background around the head and shoulders with the Eraser tool. Save and lock each document.

❖ Read *My Head Is Full of Colors* by Catherine Friend to the students and discuss.

❖ Demonstrate the following computer activity: My Head Is Full of Children.

Computer Activity

❖ Students open the documents with their cropped heads (from directions above).

❖ They select the Rubber Stamps tool. From the bottom of the screen they select a stamp that has meaning to them by clicking on it until there is a red box around it. They stamp it onto the head by clicking on the head once. They select and add more stamps to cover the top of the head. Note: View more stamps by clicking the gray arrow in the bottom right corner of the screen. (Remind students not to stamp pictures on their faces.)

❖ Students type the names of the stamps to complete this sentence from the book: "My head is full of _____."

❖ Combine all of the pages into a class book titled "My Head Is Full of Children" with your head as the cover.

How Emily Blair Got Her Fabulous Hair

based on the book by Susan Garrison

Technical Objectives

❖ import a graphic into a document

❖ crop around an image

❖ modify a graphic

❖ add text to a document

❖ use technology resources for illustration of thoughts, ideas, and stories

❖ create developmentally appropriate multimedia products

Language Arts Objectives

❖ make predictions and give support

❖ use words to describe and name objects

❖ extend a story

❖ publish written and illustrated work

Introductory Activities

❖ Scan and import a large photo of each student's head into a document. Remove the background around the head and shoulders with the Eraser tool. Save and lock each document.

❖ Read *How Emily Blair Got Her Fabulous Hair* by Susan Garrison to the students.

❖ Demonstrate the following computer activity: Hairy Scary.

Computer Activity

❖ Students open the documents with their cropped heads (from directions above).

❖ They select the Wacky Brush tool. They select a tool option from the bottom of the screen by clicking on it until there is a red box around it. They create new hair for themselves by painting on top of their heads. Note: View more Wacky Brush tool options by clicking the gray arrow in the bottom right corner of the screen.

❖ They add text to the picture: "How _____ Got His/Her Fabulous Hair" and print.

❖ Combine all of the pictures into a class book.

Extensions

❖ Ask students to write stories about how they acquired their new fabulous hair.

❖ Read the book *Camilla's New Hairdo* by Tricia Tusa. Have students use a rubber stamp as part of their new hairdos, like Camilla's Forest, Ship, and Eiffel Tower Hair.

❖ Read *Moosetache* by Margie Palatini. Use the Wacky Brush tool to create unusual hair on your head or face, just like the moose couple in the book.

How Michaela Anne Got Her Fabulous Hair

Ho for a Hat!

based on the book by William Jay Smith

Technical Objectives

❖ import a graphic into a document

❖ crop around an image

❖ modify a graphic

❖ add text to a document

❖ use input and output devices to successfully operate computers and other technologies

❖ practice responsible use of technology

❖ use technology resources for illustration of thoughts, ideas, and stories

❖ create developmentally appropriate multimedia products

Language Arts Objectives

❖ identify rhyming words

❖ identify high-frequency words

❖ identify a pattern in text

❖ write a list

❖ extend a story

❖ publish written and illustrated work

Introductory Activities

❖ Scan and import a large photo of each student's head into a document. Remove the background around the head and shoulders with the Eraser tool. Save and lock each document.

❖ Read *Ho for a Hat!* by William Jay Smith to the students. Brainstorm a list of some unusual hats that the students could create.

❖ Demonstrate the following computer project: Creating a Hat.

Computer Activity

❖ Students open the documents with their cropped heads (from directions above).

❖ They create a new hat on top of their heads using the Wacky Pencil, Rubber Stamps, or Wacky Brush tools.

❖ They add text similar to the story: "A hat _____! Ho for a Hat!" and print.

❖ Combine all of the pages into a class book.

Extensions

Share *Jennie's Hat* by Ezra Jack Keats and *Hats, Hats, Hats* by Ann Morris.

A hat can be a great place for frogs to gather!

Ho for a Hat!

Copycat Animals

based on the book by Deborah Chancellor

Technical Objectives

- ❖ import a graphic into a document
- ❖ crop around an image
- ❖ modify a graphic
- ❖ add text to a document
- ❖ use developmentally appropriate multimedia resources to support learning
- ❖ communicate about technology using developmentally appropriate and accurate terminology
- ❖ use technology resources for illustration of thoughts, ideas, and stories
- ❖ create developmentally appropriate multimedia products

Language Arts Objectives

- ❖ identify rhyming words
- ❖ use words to name and describe objects
- ❖ write simple sentences
- ❖ extend a story
- ❖ publish written and illustrated work

Introductory Activities

- ❖ Scan and import a small photo of each student's face into a document. Erase the background of each picture so only the face is showing. Save and lock each document.
- ❖ Read *Copycat Animals* by Deborah Chancellor to the students. Talk about the words used to tell about each animal in the book. Make a list of favorite animals.
- ❖ Demonstrate the following computer activity: Copycat Animals.

Computer Activity

- ❖ Students open the documents with their cropped faces.
- ❖ They use the Kid Pix tools to draw animal bodies around their faces. (Many animal rubber stamps will also work as bodies. Double-click a stamp to get to the Stamp Editor and erase the head, then stamp the body next to the head.)

❖ They use the Typewriter tool to add descriptions of the animals next to them.

❖ Print. Combine all of the pages into a class book called "Copycat Animals."

Extensions

❖ Research each animal in the book and add facts to each page.

❖ Share *Copycat Faces*, also by Deborah Chancellor. Use this book as a pattern to create your own book.

**Growl and roar.
Stand up tall**

**like a bear
upon a ball.**

Down in the Garden

based on the book by Anne Geddes

Technical Objectives

- ❖ import a graphic into a document
- ❖ crop around an image
- ❖ modify a graphic
- ❖ add text to a document
- ❖ use input and output devices to successfully operate computers and other technologies
- ❖ work collaboratively with others when using technology in the classroom
- ❖ create developmentally appropriate multimedia products

Language Arts Objectives

- ❖ use words to describe and name everyday objects
- ❖ make a list
- ❖ publish written and illustrated work
- ❖ locate information from books and nonprint materials
- ❖ write simple sentences

Introductory Activities

- ❖ Share *Down in the Garden* by Anne Geddes with the students.
- ❖ Brainstorm a list of plants and creatures that one might find in a garden.
- ❖ Take a picture of each student in the class. Crop and resize the photos until the students' faces are about 1" X 2". Save.
- ❖ Insert each photo into a new document. Erase the background of each photo until only the student's head is showing. Save and lock each document.
- ❖ Demonstrate the following computer activity: Creating a Garden Mural.

Computer Activity

- ❖ Students open the documents and transform themselves into garden plants or creatures. Print. They paint a background on a large piece of butcher paper. They cut around their computer creation and add it to the butcher paper to make a garden mural—perhaps, a *Kinder*garden.

❖ Students research and write factual information about each plant or creature to post near the mural.

Extensions

❖ Anne Geddes has also created *Down in the Garden* alphabet and counting books. Use your students' creations to create alphabet and counting books for your classroom.

❖ Study other picture book authors who use photography to illustrate their books. Examples include: Tana Hoban, Bruce McMillan, Margaret Miller, Ann Morris, Jane Bunting, Dave King, and William Wegman. How are their books similar/different? Use their books as examples for creating new class books using the digital camera and scanner.

❖ Create a *Down in the Garden* display using scanned baby pictures of your students. Ask your students to transform their photos into garden plants and animals.

Look what's GROWING.

Praise the children and they will blossom.

—Irish Proverb

Imogene's Antlers

based on the book by David Small

Technical Objectives

❖ import a graphic into a document

❖ crop around an image

❖ modify a graphic

❖ add text to a document

❖ use input and output devices to successfully operate computers and other technologies

❖ use developmentally appropriate multimedia resources to support learning

❖ use technology resources for illustration of thoughts, ideas, and stories

❖ create developmentally appropriate multimedia products

Language Arts Objectives

❖ make predictions and give support

❖ explain the problem and solution in a story

❖ write in complete sentences, using appropriate punctuation and capital letters

❖ extend a story

❖ publish written and illustrated work

Introductory Activities

❖ Read *Imogene's Antlers* by David Small to the students.

❖ Discuss the problems people might have if they woke up with an animal's features: elk antlers, an elephant trunk, a giraffe neck, eight tarantula legs, eagle wings, a pelican bill, and so on. What adaptations could be made so they could live and work in their homes?

❖ Take a picture of each student in the class. Crop and resize the pictures until the student's faces are about 1" X 2". Save.

❖ Insert each photo into a new document. Erase the background of each photo until only the student's head is showing. Save and lock each document.

❖ Demonstrate the following computer activity: Creating Animal Features.

Computer Activity

❖ Students open the documents and illustrate their pages, using themselves as the main character. They add their bodies with some features of an animal. They then add text to tell a story: "On Thursday, when _____ woke up, s/he had grown _____ . It was difficult to _____ . But s/he could _____ . On Friday, when _____ woke up, the _____ were gone. But s/he had grown _____ !" They delete the "s" in "she" if they're boys.

❖ Combine the pages into a class book.

Extensions

❖ Predict what will happen to Imogene as a peacock on Friday. Write a story as a class. What will Imogene look like on Saturday?

❖ Share *Angela's Wings* by Eric Jon Nones. What would you do if you woke up with wings like an angel?

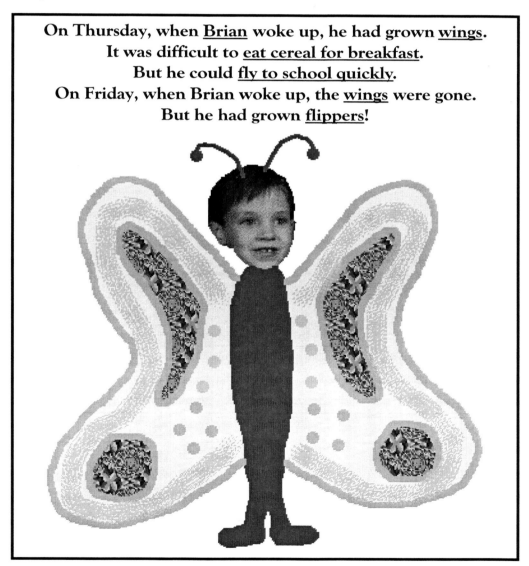

On Thursday, when <u>Brian</u> woke up, he had grown <u>wings</u>.
It was difficult to <u>eat cereal for breakfast</u>.
But he could <u>fly to school quickly</u>.
On Friday, when Brian woke up, the <u>wings</u> were gone.
But he had grown <u>flippers</u>!

Lunch

based on the book by Denise Fleming

Technical Objectives

❖ import a graphic into a document

❖ crop around an image

❖ modify a graphic

❖ add text to a document .

❖ use technology resources for directed and independent learning activities

❖ use technology resources for illustration of thoughts, ideas, and stories

❖ create developmentally appropriate multimedia products

Language Arts Objectives

❖ develop concept that print contains a message

❖ make predictions and give support

❖ use descriptive words

❖ publish written and illustrated work

Introductory Activities

❖ Read *Lunch* by Denise Fleming to the students. Talk about the adjectives used to describe the foods in the book.

❖ Brainstorm a list of words that could be used to describe various foods.

❖ Take a picture of each student in the class. Crop and resize the pictures until the students' face are about 1" X 2". Save.

❖ Insert each photo into a new document. Erase the background of each photo until only the student's head is showing. Save and lock each document.

❖ Demonstrate the following computer activity: Making Munching Mice.

Computer Activity

❖ Students open the documents and turn themselves into mice using the Kid Pix tools. They write the name of a favorite food on the screen, along with two adjectives to describe the food and print.

❖ Print the "Lunch Page 1," "Lunch End," and "Lunch Cover" templates from the disk provided. Combine these and all of the students' pages into a class book called "Lunch."

Extensions

❖ Denise Fleming's books are illustrated with handmade paper. Share some additional Denise Fleming books with your students. Then, make paper. (But don't send the handmade paper through the printer.) *Paper Making* by Marion Elliot and *The Craft of Handmade Paper* by John Plowman are good resources for this project.

❖ Insert a photo of your face over the mouse's face on the cover and end page. Add whiskers and big teeth. Cover the hair with a gray pencil so it blends with the mouse's body.

❖ This book makes a great end-of-the-year book for a teacher who is RATiring.

King Bidgood's in the Bathtub

based on the book by Audrey Wood

Technical Objectives

❖ import a graphic into a document

❖ crop around an image

❖ modify a graphic

❖ add text to a document

❖ use developmentally appropriate multimedia resources to support learning

❖ demonstrate positive social and ethical behaviors when using technology

❖ create developmentally appropriate multimedia products

Language Arts Objectives

❖ identify patterns in text

❖ make predictions and give support

❖ explain the problem and solution in a story

❖ extend a story

❖ publish written and illustrated work

Introductory Activities

❖ Read *King Bidgood's in the Bathtub* by Audrey Wood to the students. Talk about the ways that the characters in the book tried to bribe King Bidgood to get out of the bathtub.

❖ Brainstorm a list of favorite activities that the students enjoy doing. They will do these in the bathtub.

❖ Take a picture of each student in the class. Crop and resize the picture until the student's face is about 1" X 2". Save.

❖ Demonstrate the following computer activity: Who's in the Bathtub?

Computer Activity

❖ Students open the "King Bidgood" template on the disk provided. They copy and paste their photos near the bathtub on the screen. They erase the backgrounds of the photos until only their heads are showing. They move their heads closer to the bathtub using the Moving Van tool. They save and lock the documents.

❖ Students fill in the blanks in the text, based on one of their favorite activities: "Help! _____'s in the bathtub and she won't get out! Come in, said _____ with a _____, _____, _____. Today we _____ in the bathtub!" They delete the "s" in "she" if they're boys.

❖ They then illustrate their pages to match the text. They can draw a body and clothes, make water and bubbles with the Wacky Brush tool, and so on. Print.

❖ Combine all of the pages into a class book called "Who's in the Bathtub?," using the "Who's in the Bathtub? Cover" template on the disk provided.

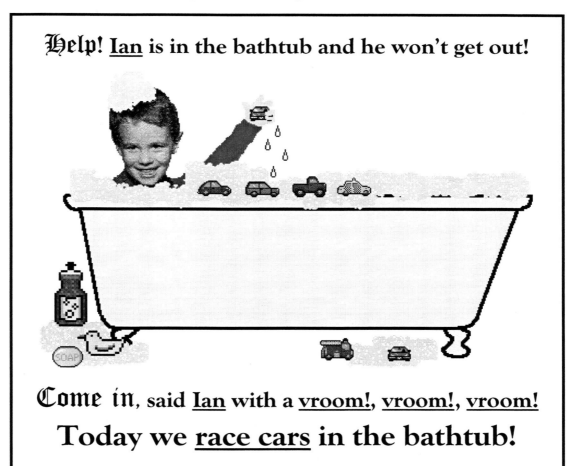

Fortunately

based on the book by Remy Charlip

Technical Objectives

❖ import a graphic into a document

❖ crop around an image

❖ modify a graphic

❖ add text to a document

❖ use technology resources for directed and independent learning activities

❖ work collaboratively with others when using technology in the classroom

❖ use technology resources for illustration of thoughts, ideas, and stories

❖ create developmentally appropriate multimedia products

Language Arts Objectives

❖ generate ideas

❖ write a list

❖ identify a pattern in a story

❖ make predictions and give support

❖ extend speaking vocabulary

❖ publish written and illustrated work

Introductory Activities

❖ Discuss the differences between "fortunate" and "unfortunate." Open the "Fortunate/Unfortunate" template on the disk provided. Brainstorm a list of events that could go in each column.

❖ Read *Fortunately* by Remy Charlip to the students. Ask the students to predict what will happen next to Ned, the main character in the story.

❖ Take a picture of each student in the class. Crop and resize each picture until the student's face is about 1" X 2". Save.

❖ Insert each photo into a new document. Erase the background of each photo until only the student's head is showing. Save and lock each document.

❖ Demonstrate the following computer activity: Fortunately/Unfortunately.

Computer Activity

❖ Students open their document and type "Fortunately _____." at the top of the screen. They type "Unfortunately _____." at the bottom of the screen. They then fill in the blanks, similar to the pattern in the story.

❖ They then illustrate the page, using themselves as the main character and print.

❖ Combine the pages into a class book called "Fortunately," using the "Fortunately Cover" template on the disk provided.

Extensions

❖ Write a Fortunately/Unfortunately story together as a class. Ask each student to word process and illustrate one page on the computer. Combine all of the pages into a book.

Fortunately Brian's mom let him paint in his room.

Unfortunately Brian painted the walls.

Curious George Goes to a Costume Party

based on the book by Margaret and H.A. Rey

Technical Objectives

❖ import a graphic into a document

❖ crop around an image

❖ modify a graphic

❖ add text to a document

❖ use input and output devices to successfully operate computers and other technologies

❖ demonstrate positive social and ethical behaviors when using technology

❖ create developmentally appropriate multimedia products

Language Arts Objectives

❖ listen to classic literature

❖ make predictions and give support

❖ explain the problem and solution in a story

❖ extend a story

❖ publish written and illustrated work

Introductory Activities

❖ Talk about costumes. When might you wear a costume? What kind of costume would you want to wear to a costume party?

❖ Read *Curious George Goes to a Costume Party* by Margaret and H.A. Rey to the students.

❖ Take a picture of each student in the class. Crop and resize each picture until the student's face is about 1" X 2". Save.

❖ Insert each photo into a new document. Erase the background of each photo until only the student's head is showing. Save and lock each document.

❖ Demonstrate the following computer activity to the students: Creating a Costume.

Computer Activity

❖ Students open their documents and create a costume for themselves using the Kid Pix tools.

Extensions

❖ Creating costumes is a fun activity to do on the computer at Halloween. Create a haunted house as a class using boxes, paint, and paper. (Add some cotton thread for creepy spiderwebs. Make tiny furniture. Design wallpaper and carpet for the house on the computer. You could even frame tiny digital photos of your students to hang on the walls.) Mount the costumed guests on tagboard and stand them up in the haunted house.

❖ Have a costume ball. Select classical music to play as a class. Tape each costumed guest to a computer's mouse. Ask each student to select a Wacky Pencil or Wacky Brush tool option. Hold down the mouse button. Make the guest on the mouse dance to the music as it plays, creating a masterpiece on the screen.

❖ Have a computer costume contest. Make ribbons on the computer to award to the winners.

Flat Stanley

based on the book by Jeff Brown

Technical Objectives

❖ take a full-length photo

❖ import a graphic into a document

❖ crop around an image

❖ modify a graphic

❖ use input and output devices to successfully operate computers and other technologies

❖ use technology resources for directed and independent learning activities

❖ use developmentally appropriate multimedia resources to support learning

❖ create developmentally appropriate multimedia products

Language Arts Objectives

❖ make predictions and give support

❖ explain the problem and solution in a story

❖ generate ideas

❖ write a list

❖ use words to describe an object

❖ write using simple sentences

❖ publish written and illustrated work

Introductory Activities

❖ Read *Flat Stanley* by Jeff Brown to the students. Talk about the activities Stanley was able to do when he was flat. Brainstorm a list of other things people could do if they were two-dimensional.

❖ Show the students a variety of paper dolls.

❖ Take a full-length body shot of each student with the digital camera. Crop and resize each photo it until it is about 4" X 5". Save.

❖ Import each picture into a Kid Pix document. Use the Eraser tool to erase around the body. Save and lock each document. These will be the students' paper dolls.

❖ Demonstrate the following computer activity: Creating Paper Dolls.

Computer Activity

❖ Students open their documents and create clothing for the dolls. They draw directly on top of their clothing in the photos. If they would like to make one or more pieces of removable clothing, they can draw clothing of an appropriate size next to the photos. They add tabs around the clothing, so that it can be attached to the paper doll, and print.

❖ They cut around the printed clothing and dolls. They mount the dolls on heavy cardboard.

❖ They write a description of the clothing to display next to the dolls.

Clothing worn in
The Story of Mercury,
a tapestry woven by
Willem van Pannemaker
in the 16th century.

Extensions

❖ Stanley's disguise, the shepherdess outfit, was from a painting in an art museum. Look at photos of famous paintings. Ask your students to dress themselves as a subject from a famous portrait.

❖ Reenact some of Stanley's activities using the paper dolls: Tie a string to the paper doll and fly it like a kite in front of a fan. Measure the paper doll in inches and centimeters. Roll up the paper doll and take it for a walk. Mail the paper doll to a friend with a note explaining the horrible bulletin board accident. Scan a landscape portrait (for scenery) and add the paper doll in front of it. Frame it.

❖ Decorate and print some of the paper dolls available in the Kid Pix cut-outs. (Select **Pick More Pictures** from the **Goodies** menu. When the Pick More Pictures dialog box opens, select the Dolls folder from the Cutouts folder. Kid Pix provides a choice of eight dolls.)

❖ Share another great picture book, *Art Dog,* by Thacher Hurd, which is about an art museum robbery.

Student Activities

Creating a Gallery

Visiting the Art Museum

based on the book by Laurene Krasny Brown and Marc Brown

Technical Objectives

- ❖ scan an image and import it into a document
- ❖ word process text to accompany the image
- ❖ use technology resources for directed and independent learning activities
- ❖ use technology resources for communication and illustration
- ❖ create developmentally appropriate multimedia products

Language Arts Objectives

- ❖ generate questions
- ❖ follow oral and written directions
- ❖ seek information using books and nonprint materials
- ❖ write a description using complete sentences
- ❖ publish written and illustrated work

Introductory Activities

- ❖ Read *Visiting the Art Museum* by Laurene Krasny Brown and Marc Brown to the students. Talk about the famous pieces that are displayed in the book. Which pieces are most interesting to the students? Which would they like to learn more about?
- ❖ Create a list of questions about the art and artists that students would like to have answered.
- ❖ Demonstrate the following computer activity: Scanning a Masterpiece.

Computer Activity

- ❖ Students select a piece of artwork from a book or museum postcard. They scan the image and import it into a new document. They write the name of the piece, the artist's name, and its location below the image.
- ❖ They write about the piece and the artist. They find the answers to the questions that were generated by the class and print.
- ❖ They cut the scanned image and text apart. They create a frame for the scanned art by following the directions in the "Frame It!" lesson. They create a class gallery in which to hang the images. They pin the information about the piece next to the picture.

Waterloo Bridge, 1900
Claude Monet
(1840–1926)
Oil on Canvas

*Photo credit: Library of Congress, Prints and Photographs
Division, Detroit Publishing Company Collection.*

Extensions

❖ Visit a local art museum. Bring your scanned images and see if you can find similar work in the museum.

❖ Stock your classroom library with art books. Lucy Micklethwait has written some wonderful books for children, illustrated with famous works of art. These include *A Child's Book of Art: Discover Great Paintings; A Child's Book of Art: Great Pictures, First Words; A Child's Book of Play in Art: Great Pictures, Great Fun; I Spy a Freight Train: Transportation in Art; I Spy a Lion: Animals in Art; I Spy: An Alphabet in Art; I Spy Two Eyes: Numbers in Art;* and *Spot a Cat.*

❖ Read *Emma* by Wendy Kesselman. Create a still life drawing using Kid Pix.

❖ Read *Milton* by Ed Massey. Scan a picture of a painting from a book or postcard. Write a story about what you think is *really* going on in the picture.

❖ Read selections from *Talking to the Sun* by Kenneth Koch and Kate Farrell. Have students scan a picture of a piece of art from another book or postcard. They select a poem that reminds them of the art and word process it next to the scanned image. Or they could write their own poems about it.

❖ Read *Matthew's Dream* by Leo Lionni. Scan a picture of a painting from a book or postcard. Have students paste a cropped photo of themselves or a friend onto the painting. They modify the photo so that they become part of the painting. They write about their adventures.

❖ Check the local library and computer store for art galleries on CD. *With Open Eyes* is a CD collection that is very appropriate for young students.

Visiting the Art Museum—Online!

Technical Objectives

❖ copy and paste graphics and text

❖ gather information and communicate with others using telecommunications

❖ use technology resources for directed and independent learning activities

❖ demonstrate positive social and ethical behaviors using technology

❖ create developmentally appropriate multimedia products

Language Arts Objectives

❖ follow directions

❖ use technology to locate information

❖ write simple sentences

❖ publish written and illustrated work

Introductory Activities

❖ Demonstrate how to access The Art Institute of Chicago online (www.artic.edu/aic/collections/index.html). You may wish to save the address as a bookmark or make it your home page so students can get to it more quickly.

❖ Go to the site. Click Collections. View some of the artwork by clicking the View Art, Explore (Galleries), and Discover (Exhibitions) buttons. Show how to move back and forward, so students can maneuver between the three areas.

❖ Select one picture to print and frame. Move the pointer onto the picture. Hold down the mouse button. When a menu appears, select **Copy This Image** and release the mouse button.

Note from the author and publisher: We checked with The Art Institute of Chicago and were told that this use of their Web site is legal as long as the images are captured for classroom use only. We are not able to show an example from the Web site for this activity without licensing the image for this book.

❖ Open a new document. Select **Paste** from the **Edit** menu. Move the image to the desired spot on the screen. Save the document.

❖ Return to The Art Institute of Chicago site. Highlight the description of the artwork by dragging the mouse over the words. Copy and paste the words under the picture in the document.

❖ Return to The Art Institute of Chicago site. Highlight the Internet address at the top of the screen. Copy and paste the address (your source) under the description.

Computer Activity

❖ Students access The Art Institute of Chicago online (www.artic.edu/aic/collections/index.html). They copy and paste one picture from the Web site.

❖ They copy and paste the name of the piece, the artist's name, its location, and the site address below the image.

❖ They locate information about the piece or its creator from the Internet, books, or other sources.

❖ They write about the piece or the artist.

❖ They print and cut out the image and the caption.

❖ They create a frame for the picture by following the directions in the "Frame It!" lesson. They create a class gallery in which to hang the images. They pin the information about each piece next to the corresponding picture. They participate in a gallery tour.

Extensions

❖ Visit other museums on the Web. All of the following museums feature famous artwork and special exhibitions. Most also offer museum tours.

American Museum of Photography
www.photographymuseum.com

Metropolitan Museum of Art
www.metmuseum.org

Museum of Fine Arts, Boston
www.mfa.org/home.htm

The Louvre, Paris
http://mistral.culture.fr/louvre/louvrea.htm

ArtNet Gallery (links to museums)
http://artnetgallery.com/links.html

Frame It!

When we capture a special image with a standard camera, we tend to frame it and display it. Why should it be any different when using a digital camera (or scanner or graphics program)? Let students display their work from the computer creatively. Frame the work and create a gallery in your classroom.

There are several ways to create borders, frames, and mattes in Kid Pix.

❖ Decorate the entire screen using one or several of the tools. Go all the way to the outside edge. Mix the colors into a pattern with the Electric Mixer tool, if you choose. Select the Rectangle or Oval tool. At the bottom of the screen, select the second tool option. Draw a large rectangle or oval over the pattern. This will create a patterned frame around the outside of the screen into which to insert the photo.

❖ Insert the photo into a new document. Draw a rectangle around it to create the outside of a frame. Select a pattern from the Paint Can tool options. Color the space between the photo and the rectangle.

❖ Select the Wacky Brush tool. Paint a border around the outside of the photo using a favorite tool option. (Copy and paste portions to keep the pattern aligned.) The Log Cabin tool option works really well for creating straight borders.

❖ Select the Wacky Brush tool. Select the Dotty Frame, Photo Album, Animals Frame, Open Window, or Roll of Film tool option. These will create a frame into which to import the photo.

❖ Use the Rubber Stamps tool to stamp a border around the outside of the photo (or customize a patterned border with some rubber stamps). You can choose animals, foods, plants, monsters, and so on. The Toonies 2, Write Away, and Western sets of stamps also have neat patterns that can be stamped together to make a border.

❖ Insert the photo into an enlarged rubber stamp. There are a few frames and screens hidden within the sets of rubber stamps that can be enlarged and used as frames and borders. The Hodgepodge and Fantasy sets of stamps each have a frame. Fantasy also has a mirror and a crystal ball into which to copy and paste a photo. The Original stamp set has a computer screen, and Toonies 1 has a TV monitor. Display the photo using a variety of stamps ... be creative.

Just as there are several ways to create borders, frames, and mattes in Kid Pix, there are also several ways to use them.

❖ Copy and paste the photo inside the frame before you print it, creating a 2-D display. This is an especially attractive way to frame work that will be compiled into a class book. Many picture books use borders as part of their illustrations. *Whoever You Are* by Mem Fox, *Baby Rattlesnake* by Lynn Moroney, *Feelings* by Janie Spaht Gill, and *Simon's Book* by Henrik Drescher are good examples of books with borders to share with students.

❖ Print the borders that your students create and add their work later. This allows the students to decorate their borders more easily and creatively. The students' Kid Pix borders can be glued directly onto wooden or cardboard frames. Display their computer work behind the frames.

❖ Print the students' borders. Cut, embellish, and use them as mattes to place inside frames. The frames used with these mattes can be purchased at a store or created by the students themselves. For some creative ideas on making picture frames with your students, read *Decorative Frames* by Miranda Innes and *Making and Decorating Picture Frames* by Janet Bridge.

Framing and attractively displaying your students' work will give your students and their work the recognition they deserve. Make sure the gallery contains a variety of work: portraits, group photos, landscapes, action, and still life. You can also create a gallery of famous work using the scanner, the Internet, and the resources in the "Visiting the Art Museum" lesson.

Digital Camera and Scanner Links
across the Curriculum

The skills your students have acquired using the digital camera and scanner can be applied in all subject areas and tied to any piece of literature. Just be creative. For example:

Literature Links!

Scan book covers to add to book reports.

Scan book characters. Cut them out and turn them into puppets for a play.

Crop around your face and turn yourself into a character from a favorite book.

Design letterhead for favorite book characters and write letters from their perspectives.

History in the Making!

Crop around your face. Dress yourself for the time period you're studying.

Scan pictures of historical figures. Create a timeline to put the people into perspective.

Math Madness!

❖ Graph photos of your students according to various traits.

❖ Create a counting book by taking pictures of groups of objects.

❖ Use photography to inspire discussion and investigation about length, depth, symmetry, and angles.

Science SlideShows!

❖ Photograph or scan the stages of a science experiment, or plant or animal growth. Bring the images into Kid Pix and write about them. Create a Kid Pix SlideShow about the topic.

❖ Try experiments from Chris Oxlade's book *Cameras*. Learn about recording, printing, and projecting images; using lenses, light, and filters; focal lengths; and animation.

Digital Art!

❖ Experiment with photomontage, a technique in which photos are cut apart, carefully overlapped and pieced together in a new way.

❖ Use photography as a means to teach display techniques.

❖ Study a variety of photographers and their work. Invite a photographer to visit your classroom and share tips with students.

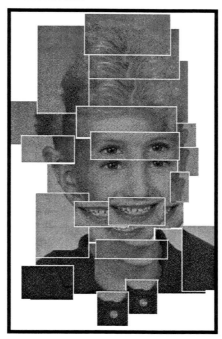

Movement and Music!

❖ What better time to practice taking action shots.

❖ Invite a sports photographer to visit your classroom and share tips with your students.

❖ Scan photos of favorite musicians and write about them.

❖ Scan pictures of instruments. Ask your students to name the instruments and identify their sounds in music.

❖ Take pictures of your students in action to import into weekly newsletters, progress reports, yearbooks, or program covers.

Appendix

National Standards

The lessons in this book meet a variety of national standards in technology, visual arts, and primary language arts. The following pages provide the achievement standards for early elementary students in each content area.

International Society for Technology in Education
National Educational Technology Standards (NETS) for Students

The Kid Pix Digital Gallery lessons meet the national technology standards. Most of the following standards are satisfied daily by using technology individually and collaboratively in the classroom, imitating adults modeling appropriate behavior, and discussing important issues in technology. Read the Technical Objectives section at the beginning of each lesson plan to see specific objectives for each lesson.

NETS for Students

1. Basic operations and concepts

   ❖ Students demonstrate a sound understanding of the nature and operation of technology systems.

   ❖ Students are proficient in the use of technology.

2. Social, ethical, and human issues

   ❖ Students understand the ethical, cultural, and societal issues related to technology.

   ❖ Students practice responsible use of technology systems, information, and software.

   ❖ Students develop positive attitudes toward technology uses that support lifelong learning, collaboration, personal pursuits, and productivity.

3. Technology productivity tools

❖ Students use technology tools to enhance learning, increase productivity, and promote creativity.

❖ Students use productivity tools to collaborate in constructing technology-enhanced models, preparing publications, and producing other creative works.

4. Technology communications tools

❖ Students use telecommunications to collaborate, publish, and interact with peers, experts, and other audiences.

❖ Students use a variety of media and formats to communicate information and ideas effectively to multiple audiences.

5. Technology research tools

❖ Students use technology to locate, evaluate, and collect information from a variety of sources.

❖ Students use technology tools to process data and report results.

❖ Students evaluate and select new information resources and technological innovations based on the appropriateness to specific tasks.

6. Technology problem-solving and decision-making tools

❖ Students use technology resources for solving problems and making informed decisions.

❖ Students employ technology in the development of strategies for solving problems in the real world.

Performance Indicators:

Numbers in parentheses following each performance indicator refer to the standards category to which the performance is linked.

Prior to Completion of Grade 2 students will:

1. Use input devices (e.g., mouse, keyboard, remote control) and output devices (e.g., monitor, printer) to successfully operate computers, VCRs, audiotapes, and other technologies. (1)

2. Use a variety of media and technology resources for directed and independent learning activities. (1, 3)

3. Communicate about technology using developmentally appropriate and accurate terminology. (1)

4. Use developmentally appropriate multimedia resources (e.g., interactive books, educational software, elementary multimedia encyclopedias) to support learning. (1)

5. Work cooperatively and collaboratively with peers, family members, and others when using technology in the classroom. (2)

6. Demonstrate positive social and ethical behaviors when using technology. (2)

7. Practice responsible use of technology systems and software. (2)

8. Create developmentally appropriate multimedia products with support from teachers, family members, or student partners. (3)

9. Use technology resources (e.g., puzzles, logical thinking programs, writing tools, digital cameras, drawing tools) for problem solving, communication, and illustration of thoughts, ideas, and stories. (3, 4, 5, 6)

10. Gather information and communicate with others using telecommunications, with support from teachers, family members, or student partners. (4)

The National Educational Technology Standards for Students *(June 1998) are reprinted with permission. NETS is published by ISTE (International Society for Technology in Education, NETS Project). The full document is available from ISTE at 800.336.5191 (U.S. and Canada) or 541.302.3777 (International) and on the Web at www.iste.org (select Standards Projects).*

National Art Education Association
K–4 Visual Arts Standards

Many visual arts standards are met in Kid Pix Digital Gallery. *The concepts presented and correlating Kid Pix projects help to satisfy many of the Achievement Standards on the following pages.*

1. **Content Standard: Understanding and applying media, techniques, and processes**

   Achievement Standard:
   Students

   a. know the differences between materials, techniques, and processes

   b. describe how different materials, techniques, and processes cause different responses

   c. use different media, techniques, and processes to communicate ideas, experiences, and stories

   d. use art materials and tools in a safe and responsible manner

2. **Content Standard: Using knowledge of structures and functions**

   Achievement Standard:
   Students

   a. know the differences among visual characteristics and purposes of art in order to convey ideas

   b. describe how different expressive features and organizational principles cause different responses

   c. use visual structures and functions of art to communicate ideas

3. **Content Standard: Choosing and evaluating a range of subject matter, symbols, and ideas**

   Achievement Standard:
   Students

   a. explore and understand prospective content for works of art

   b. select and use subject matter, symbols, and ideas to communicate meaning

4. Content Standard: Understanding the visual arts in relation to history and cultures

   Achievement Standard:
   Students

   a. know that the visual arts have both a history and specific relationships to various cultures

   b. identify specific works of art as belonging to particular cultures, times, and places

   c. demonstrate how history, culture, and the visual arts can influence each other in making and studying works of art

5. Content Standard: Reflecting upon and assessing the characteristics and merits of their work and the work of others

   Achievement Standard:
   Students

   a. understand there are various purposes for creating works of visual art

   b. describe how people's experiences influence the development of specific artworks

   c. understand there are different responses to specific artworks

6. Content Standard: Making connections between visual arts and other disciplines

   Achievement Standard:
   Students

   a. understand and use similarities and differences between characteristics of the visual arts and other arts disciplines

   b. identify connections between the visual arts and other disciplines in the curriculum

Reprinted with permission from The National Visual Arts Standards, *Copyright 1994, by the National Art Education Association.*

International Reading Association (IRA) and National Council of Teachers of English (NCTE) Standards for the English Language Arts

The activities in Kid Pix Digital Gallery *meet the broad language arts standards on the following pages. Please note that the language arts standards cannot be separated. They are interrelated and should be considered as a whole. For practical use, I have listed more specific Language Arts Objectives in the section at the beginning of each lesson plan. Please read these objectives to see how the lesson fits into the IRA/NCTE standards.*

1. Students read a wide range of print and nonprint texts to build an understanding of texts, of themselves, and of the cultures of the United States and the world; to acquire new information; to respond to the needs and demands of society and the workplace; and for personal fulfillment. Among these texts are fiction and nonfiction, classic and contemporary works.

2. Students read a wide range of literature from many periods in many genres to build an understanding of the many dimensions (e.g., philosophical, ethical, and aesthetic) of human experience.

3. Students apply a wide range of strategies to comprehend, interpret, evaluate, and appreciate texts. They draw on their prior experiences, their interactions with other readers and writers, their knowledge of word meaning and of other texts, their word identification strategies, and their understanding of textual features (e.g., sound-letter correspondence, sentence structure, context, and graphics).

4. Students adjust their use of spoken, written, and visual language (e.g., conventions, style, and vocabulary) to communicate effectively with a variety of audiences and for different purposes.

5. Students employ a wide range of strategies as they write and use different writing process elements appropriately to communicate with different audiences for a variety of purposes.

6. Students apply knowledge of language structure, language conventions (e.g., spelling and punctuation), media techniques, figurative language, and genre to create critique, and discuss print and nonprint texts.

7. Students conduct research on issues and interests by generating ideas and questions, and by posing problems. They gather, evaluate, and synthesize data from a variety of sources (e.g., print and nonprint texts, artifacts, and people) to communicate their discoveries in ways that suit their purpose and audience.

8. Students use a variety of technological and informational resources (e.g., libraries, databases, computer networks, and video) to gather and synthesize information and to create and communicate knowledge.

9. Students develop an understanding of and respect for diversity in language use, patterns, and dialects across cultures, ethnic groups, geographic regions, and social roles.

10. Students whose first language is not English make use of their first language to develop competency in the English language arts and to develop understanding of content across the curriculum.

11. Students participate as knowledgeable, reflective, creative, and critical members of a variety of literacy communities.

12. Students use spoken, written, and visual language to accomplish their own purposes (e.g., for learning, enjoyment, persuasion, and the exchange of information).

Reprinted with permission from Standards for the English Language Arts, *p. 24, Copyright 1996, by the International Reading Association and National Council of Teachers of English. All Rights Reserved.*

List of Books for Activities

Blos, Joan W. *The Grandpa Days*. Simon and Schuster, 1989.

Bridge, Janet. *Making and Decorating Picture Frames*. North Light Books, 1996.

Brown, Jeff. *Flat Stanley*. Scholastic Books, 1964.

Brown, Laurene Krasny, and Brown, Marc. *Visiting the Art Museum*. E.P. Dutton, 1986.

Bucknall, Caroline. *One Bear in the Picture*. Dial Books for Young Readers, 1988.

Bunting, Eve. *Flower Garden*. Harcourt Brace and Company, 1994.

Bunting, Jane. *My First ABC*. DK Publishing, 1993.

Bunting, Jane. *My First Action Word Book*. DK Publishing, 1996.

Caple, Kathy. *Harry's Smile*. Houghton Mifflin Company, 1987.

Castle, Caroline, and Bowman, Peter. *Grandpa Baxter and the Photographs*. Orchard Books, 1993.

Chancellor, Deborah. *Copycat Animals*. DK Publishing, 1999.

Chancellor, Deborah. *Copycat Faces*. DK Publishing, 1999.

Charlip, Remy. *Fortunately*. McMillan Publishing Company, 1993.

Cox, Rhonda. *Click!* Richard C. Owen Publishers, Inc., 1997.

Dragonwagon, Crescent. *Alligators and Others All Year Long: A Book of Months*. Macmillan Publishing Company, 1993.

Drescher, Henrik. *Simon's Book*. Lothrop, Lee and Shepherd Books, 1983.

Drew, David. *Animal Clues*. Rigby Inc., 1987.

Drew, David. *Mystery Monsters*. Rigby Inc., 1987.

Elliot, Marion. *Paper Making*. Henry Holt and Company, 1994.

Everett, Janie, *Faces*. Scott Foresman, 1993.

Fleming, Denise. *Lunch*. Henry Holt and Company, 1992.

Fox, Mem. *Whoever You Are*. Harcourt Brace and Company, 1997.

Friend, Catherine. *My Head Is Full of Colors*. Hyperion, 1994.

Gage, Amy Glaser. *Pascual's Magic Pictures*. Carolrhoda Books, Inc., 1996.

Garrison, Susan. *How Emily Blair Got Her Fabulous Hair*.
Bridgewater Books, 1995.

Geddes, Anne. *Down in the Garden*, Cedco Publishing Company, 1996.

Gibbons, Gail. *Click! A Book about Cameras and Taking Pictures*. Little, Brown
and Company, 1997.

Gill, Janie Spaht. *Feelings*. ARO Publishing, 1998.

Hafner, Marilyn. *A Year with Molly and Emmett*. Candlewick Press, 1997.

Hague, Kathleen. *Calendarbears*. Henry Holt and Company, 1997.

Harrison, Joanna. *Dear Bear*. Carolrhoda Books, 1994.

Hoban, Lillian. *Arthur's Pen Pal*. Harper and Row Publishers, 1976.

Hoban, Tana. *Just Look*. Greenwillow Books, 1996.

Hoban, Tana. *Look Again!* McMillan, 1971.

Hoban, Tana. *Look Book*. Greenwillow Books, 1997.

Hoban, Tana. *Look! Look! Look!* Greenwillow Books, 1988.

Hoban, Tana. *Take Another Look*. Greenwillow Books, 1981.

Hurd, Thacher. *Art Dog*. Harper Collins Publishers, 1996.

Innes, Miranda. *Decorative Frames*. Dorling Kindersley, 1995.

Keats, Ezra Jack. *Jennie's Hat*. Harper and Row Publishers, 1966.

Kesselman, Wendy. *Emma*. Harper and Row Publishers, 1980.

Kindersley, Barnabas, and Kindersley, Anabel. *Children Just Like Me: A Unique
Celebration of Children around the World*. DK Publishing, 1995.

King, Dave. *Alphabet Book*. DK Publishing, 1997.

King, Dave. *Counting Book*. DK Publishing, 1998.

King, Dave. *My First Photography Book*. DK Publishing, 1994.

Koch, Kenneth, and Farrell, Kate. *Talking to the Sun: An Illustrated Anthology of Poems for Young People*. Henry Holt and Company, 1985.

Lionni, Leo. *Matthew's Dream*. Alfred A. Knopf, 1991.

Marshall, Janet Perry. *My Camera at the Aquarium*. Little, Brown and Company, 1989.

Marshall, Janet Perry. *My Camera at the Zoo*. Little, Brown and Company, 1989.

Massey, Ed. *Milton*. Wetlands Press, 1995.

Math Workshop. Brøderbund Software, 1995.

McMillan, Bruce. *Mouse Views*. Holiday House, 1993.

McPhail, David. *Pig Pig and the Magic Photo Album*. E.P. Dutton, 1986.

Micklethwait, Lucy. *A Child's Book of Art: Discover Great Paintings*. Dorling Kindersley, 1999.

Micklethwait, Lucy. *A Child's Book of Art: Great Pictures, First Words*. Dorling Kindersley, 1993.

Micklethwait, Lucy. *A Child's Book of Play in Art: Great Pictures, Great Fun*. Dorling Kindersley, 1996.

Micklethwait, Lucy. *I Spy: An Alphabet in Art*. Greenwillow Books, 1992.

Micklethwait, Lucy. *I Spy a Freight Train: Transportation in Art*. Greenwillow Books, 1996.

Micklethwait, Lucy. *I Spy a Lion: Animals in Art*. Greenwillow Books, 1994.

Micklethwait, Lucy. *I Spy Two Eyes: Numbers in Art*. Greenwillow Books, 1993.

Micklethwait, Lucy. *Spot a Cat*. Dorling Kindersley, 1995.

Moore, Elaine. *Grandma's Promise*. Lothrop, Lee and Shepard Books, 1988.

Moroney, Lynn. *Baby Rattlesnake*. Children's Book Press, 1989.

Morris, Ann. *Hats, Hats, Hats*. Lothrop, Lee and Shepard Books, 1989.

Munsch, Robert. *Love You Forever*. Firefly Books, 1986.

Nelson, Nan Ferring. *My Day with Anka*. Lothrop, Lee and Shepard Books, 1996.

Nigel's World Geography, Lawrence Productions, 1991.

Nones, Eric Jon. *Angela's Wings*. Farrar, Straus, Giroux, 1995.

Oxlade, Chris. *Cameras*. Gareth Stevens Publishing, 1997.

Palatini, Margie. *Moosetache*. Hyperion Books for Children, 1997.

Plowman, John. *The Craft of Handmade Paper*. Knickerbocker Press, 1997.

Polacco, Patricia. *Appelemando's Dreams*. Philomel Books, 1991.

Priddy, Roger. *My Big Book of Everything*. DK Publishing, 1996.

Reading Rainbow. Lancit Media Productions Ltd., GPN & WNED-TV.

Rey, Margaret, and Rey, H.A. *Curious George Goes to a Costume Party*. Houghton Mifflin Company, 1986.

Root, Betty. *My First Dictionary*. DK Publishing, 1993.

Scott, Ann Herbert. *Grandmother's Chair*. Clarion Books, 1990.

Small, David. *Imogene's Antlers*. Crown Publishers, Inc., 1985.

Smith, William Jay. *Ho for a Hat!* Little, Brown and Company, 1989.

Tucker, Jean S. *Come Look With Me: Discovering Photographs with Children*. Thomasson-Grant, Inc., 1994.

Tusa, Tricia. *Camilla's New Hairdo*. Farrar, Straus, Giroux, 1991.

Watson, Carol. *My First Encyclopedia*. DK Publishing, 1993.

Willard, Nancy. *Simple Pictures Are Best*. Harcourt, Brace, Jovanovich, 1976.

Wolff, Ferida. *A Year for Kiko*. Houghton Mifflin Company, 1997.

Wood, Audrey. *King Bidgood's in the Bathtub*. Harcourt, Brace, Jovanovich Publishers, 1985.

Ziebel, Peter. *Look Closer*. Clarion Books, 1989.

Ziefert, Harriet. *My Camera*. Harriet Ziefert, Inc., 1993.

References

Alden, S.B. (1998, September). The role technology can play in preparing our children for the 21st century. [Online]. Available: http://computerlearning.org/Articles/Prepare.htm

Catchings, M.H., & MacGregor, K. (1998, March). Stoking creative fires: Young authors use software for writing and illustrating. *Learning & Leading with Technology, 25.*

International Reading Association (IRA) and National Council of Teachers of English (NCTE). (1996). *Standards for the English language arts.* Urbana, IL: Authors.

International Society for Technology in Education. (1998). *National educational technology standards for students.* [Brochure]. Eugene, OR: Author.

Jankowski, L. (1998, March). Educational computing: Why use a computer for writing? *Learning & Leading with Technology, 25.*

National Art Education Association. (1994). *The national visual arts standards.* Reston, VA: Author.